TOWARD A RA INTERPRETATION OF THE ABRAHAMIC RELIGIONS: IN SEARCH FOR THE WHOLLY OTHER

Rudolf J. Siebert
Professor of Religion and Society

Western Michigan University
Kalamazoo, Michigan
2012

S
Sanbun Publishers
New Delhi

© Sanbun Publishers 2012

ISBN: 978-93-82393-11-5

S

Sanbun Publishers
403 Imperial Tower, Naraina Commercial Centre,
C-Block Naraina Vihar, New Delhi-110028
Tel.   : 98101-94729
E-mail : sanbunpublishers@hotmail.com

Library Cataloguing

Siebert, Prof. Rudolf, Toward a Radical..., S.C., Pg. 160, Rs.150.00, US $14.95, 2012

Typeset in 10pt Palatino by Golden Printographics, New Delhi
Printed and bound by ABC Press, New Delhi

Gratefully to my daughter
Agnes Maria

Toward a Radical Naturalistic and Humanistic Interpretation of the Abrahamic Religions: In Search for the Wholly Other than the Horror and Terror of Nature and History

According to the Rabbis, the modern antagonism between the sacred and the profane, or between the religious and the secular, had been unknown to the Torah as - so the dialectical religiologist may add - to any other ancient sacred writing (Leviticus 19:2; 20:7-9, 10-12; Lieber 2001: 693, 701-702; Hegel 1965; 1969; 1972; 1986j; 1986p: 9-88; 1986q; 1986r; 1986s; 1986t; Marx 2000; Otto 1969; 1991; Eliade 1961; Adorno 1963; 1969a; 1969b; 1993c; Küng 1978; 1991b; Benedict XVI 2011; Williams 2011:127-154;Maciejewski 2919;Lohmann 2011:71-72). Everything we do, so the Rabbis thought, had the potential of being holy, and according to the Torah and the Talmud those people, who thought that there was no God, and that the world of nature and of man - family, society, state, history and culture - was entirely secular and profane, were considered to be foolish, false, corrupt, vile, evil, unwise, tainted, ignorant, stupid, unclean, impure, lawless, immoral, wicked, evildoers, and they were seen as apostates, and they were struck by fear without reason, and their bones were scattered, and they were disgraced, and they were rejected by God and the community of the believers, and they were forgotten (Levitcus 21; 22; Psalm 53; 91; 92; Lieber 2001: 717-724; John 13: 1- 20, esp.; 10-11; Hegel 1096 g; 1986l; 1986p; 1986q; Küng 1991b).

I. Holiness

In the Rabbis' perspective, to be *holy* was to be different, to be set apart from the ordinary life of the people (Leviticus 19:2; 20:7-9, 10-12; 21; 22 Ezekiel 20:2-20;44:15-31 Lieber 2001: 693, 701-702, 713-714, 717-724;734-735).. The *ordinary* was often used as the opposite of *holy*. In Rabbinic discourse, to be holy was to rise to partake in some measure of the special qualities of God, the source of holiness. Holiness was the highest of human behavior: human beings at their most Godlike. Martin Buber wrote, that Judaism did not divide life, as modern people do, into the holy and the profane: but rather into the holy and the not-yet-holy (Lieber 2001: 693; Bloch 1985c; 1985d; 1985e; 2009; Kogon 1965; 1967; 1995; 2002; 2003a; 2003b). Similarly Finkelstone wrote, that Judaism is a way of life, that endeavors to transform virtually every human action into a means of communion with God (Lieber 2001: 693). The Talmud enunciated the important principle of achieving holiness within the realm of the permitted. Jews were supposed to go beyond obeying the letter of the law, and refraining from what was forbidden, by finding ways of sanctifying every moment in their lives. People could be as holy as they allowed themselves to be. Ramban warned against the person, who managed to lead an unworthy life without technically breaking any of the Torah's rules. Such a person was called a scoundrel within the bounds of the Torah (Leviticus 19:2; Lieber 2001: 693). In the Rabbi's view, the capacity for holiness was not restricted to spiritually gifted people. Anyone may attain holiness. God did not demand the impossible. There was nobody who was religiously entirely unmusical, as Max Weber and Jürgen Habermas assumed: everybody could become old and pious (Weber 1952; 1962; 1963; 1969; 1978; 1992; Arens 2009). The critical theorist of religion observes, that traditional societies are not only opposed to the profanization of the sacred, but rather try to overcome and reconcile the difference between the religious and the secular through the progressive sanctification of the profane, or through de-secularization (Leviticus 19: 12. Lieber 2001: 695/12; Hegel 1986p; 1986q; Küng 1970; 1978; 1981a; 1990b; 1991a; 1991b; 1994a; 2004; Küng/Ess/Stietencron/ Bechel 1984; Küng/Homolka 2009; Küng/Kuschel 1993a; 1993b; Kuschel 1990; Kuschel/Schlensog 2008; Metz/ Wiesel 1993; Karpov 2010: 232-270; Byrd 2011; Ferguson 2010; Moore 2009; Benedict XVI 2011; Siebert 2010b). The relationship between the sacred and the profane is extremely dialectical (Hegel 1986p; 1986q; Küng 1978; 1991b; 1994a; 1994b; 2004; Benedict XVI 2011).

Community

In the view of the Rabbis, holiness was most easily achieved in the context of a religious community (Leviticus 19:2; Lieber 2001: 693; Dirks 1968; 1983a; 1983b; 1985; 1987; 1988; Metz 1978; 1980; Metz/Habermas/Sölle 1994; Metz/Peters 1991; Metz/Rendtorf 1971; Metz/Wiesel 1993; Küng 1991; 1994; 2004; 1991b; 1994a; 1994b; 2004; 2009 Benedict XVI 2011). It was difficult for a person to live a life of holiness without others. According to the Torah, Noah was not able to do it. (Exodus 6-9). Even Abraham lapsed into unworthy behavior, when surrounded by people, who were not striving for holiness, as he was (Genesis 12:20). When a community dedicated itself to the pursuit of holiness, its members supported and reinforced each other Historically, when Jewish - or Christian, or Islamic, or Buddhist, or Hindu, etc. - communities have been at their best, the whole became greater than the sum of its parts (Leviticus 19:2; Lieber 2001: 693; Hegel 1965; 1969; 1972; 1986j; 1996p. 1986q:329-344; 1986r; 1986s; 1986t; Otto 1969; 1991; Dirks 1968; 1983a; 1983b; 1985; 1987; 1988; Metz 1978; 1980; Metz/ Habermas/Sölle 1994; Metz/Peters 1991; Metz/Rendtorf 1971; Metz/Wiesel 1993; Küng 1978; 1990b; 1991a; 1991b; Küng/Ess/Stietencron/Bechert 1984; Küng/Homolka 2009; Küng/Kuschel 1993b; Kuschel 1990; Kuschel/Schlensog 2008; Benedict XVI 2011). Ordinary people achieved an extraordinary measure of sanctity in their daily lives. The divine commandment *You shall be holy* has been understood by some Rabbis not as a command, but as a promise (Leviticus 19:2; Lieber 2001: 693; Hegel 1965; 1969; 1972; 1986j; 1096p. 1986q; 1986r; 1986s; 1986t; Otto 1969; 1991; Küng 1978; 1991b; Benedict XVI 2011). Hatam Sofer promised: Live by these rules and your life will become special in the process (Leviticus 19:2; Lieber 2001: 694). Your fundamental need for significance, for the assurance that your life has meaning, will be met thereby. For Heschel, Judaism was an attempt to prove, that in order to be a man you have to be more than a man, that in order to be a people, you have to be more than a people. Israel had been made to be a holy people. In the perspective of the dialectical religiology, secular socialist humanism determinately negates -i. e. criticizes, but also preserves, elevates, and tries to fulfill - positive religion, particularly the ethical theism of the three Abrahamic religions in terms of a post-theistic religiosity or spirituality (Hegel 1986p; 1986q; Fromm 1932a; 1932b; 1950; 1956; 1957; 1959; 1961; 1964; 1966a; 1966b; 1966c; 1967; 1968; 1970a; 1970b; 1972a; 1972b; 1973; 1974; 1976; 1980b; 1981; 1990a; 1990b; 1992; 1995; 1997; 1999; 2001; Funk 1995; 1999; 2000a; 2000b; Funk/ Joach/Meuer 2000; Fromm/ SuzukiMartino 1960; Fromm/ Xirau 1979; Tillich 1926; 1929; 1933; 1948; 1951; 1952; 19545a; 1955b; 1957; 1963a; 1963b; 1966; 1972; 1977; 1983; Fuegi

1994; Küng 1970; 1978; 1981a; 1982; 1990a; 1990b; 1991a; 1991b; 1994a; 2004; Küng/Ess/Stietencron/ Bechel 1984; Küng/Homolka 2009; Küng/Kuschel 1993a; 1993b; Kuschel 1990; Kuschel/Schlensog 2008; Benedict XVI 2011; Metz/ Wiesel 1993; Fuhr 2003; : 17-18; 2004a: 24-27; 2004b; 20-23; Zizek 2007; 2009; Zizek/Milbank 2008; Byrd 2011; Siebert 2010b).

II. Disharmony

According to the critical theory of religion, the modern not only difference, but outright antagonism, disharmony, and dissonance between the sacred and the profane, the religious and the secular, revelation and enlightenment, faith and reason, which had been unknown to the Torah and the Jewish community as well as to any other traditional society, had started in the Western civilization alone with the Renaissance and the Reformation, with the discoveries of Copernicus, and of Galilei Galileo, and of Isaac Newton, and of Rene Descartes, and reached a climax after the bourgeois enlightenment movements and revolutions in England, France, and America and with the Marxian enlightenment and the socialist revolutions (Leviticus 19:2; Lieber 2001: 693; Hegel 1965; 1969; 1972; 1986a: 47; 1986b: 184, 263; 1986d: 427, 292, 306, 323, 341- 342, 345 431; 1986e: 298-299, 303, 307-309 320, 337, 369, 406, 407, 434; 1986f: 402; 1986g: 426; 1986h: 154-155, 158; 165-167, 148; 1986i: 78-79, 94; 1986j; 1986l: 491-542; 1986p; 1986q; 1986r; 1986s; 1986t:42; Marx 1871; 1906; 1951; 1953; 1956; 1961a; 1961b; 1961c; 1963 1964; 1974; 1977; 2000; Marc/ Engels 2005; Lenin 1972; Otto1969; 1991; Eliade 1961; Adorno 1963; 1969a; 1969b; 1996; Brecht 1966; Küng 1978; 1991b;Kesting 2011: 68-70). Around 1800, Hegel recognized in European culture three stages or estates of modernization and secularization:
1. The first stage of the immediate and naïve religion and faith.

2. The second estate of the analytical understanding of the so called educated people, of reflection and enlightenment.
3. The third stage of dialectical philosophy as theology, in which religion and reason had been reconciled for philosophers by the power of the dialectical notion - the self-particularization or self-estrangement, and the self- singularization or self-reconciliation of the universal - but not for the masses of the people living in civil society, not for the average bourgeois, not to speak of the proletarian.

(Hegel 1964; 1965; 1969; 1972; 1979; 1986c; 1986e; 1986f; 1986g: 339-397; 1986l; 1986q: 342-344; Marx 1871; 1906; 1951; 1953: chap. VI, X; Lefebvre 1982 Moore 2009; Ferguson 2010). When Hegel looked at the origin, and the existence, and the full development and realization of the Christian community at the beginning of the 19th century, and saw finally its spiritual reality fall into this threefold disunion of estates or stages, then it appeared to him, that this its realization was at the same time its passing away, its destruction. But the Lutheran Hegel asked himself, if he could really speak in all seriousness of the going under of the Christian community, since according to the Christian revelation and faith the *Kingdom of God* was grounded for eternity, and the *Holy Spirit* lived as such eternally in his community, and the powers of hell could not possibly overcome the Church (Revelation 21-22; Hegel 1986q: 342-344; Küng 1970; 1972; 1976; 1978; 1980; 1994a; 1994b; Moore 2009; Ferguson 2010; Benedict XVI 2011). Hegel was fully aware, that to speak about the passing away of the Church, meant to end his whole philosophy of religion with a *disharmony* not only for Christianity, but for all the other still living world-religions as well (Hegel 1986p; 1986q; Hegel 1965; 1969; 1972; 1986j; 1986p; 1986q; 1986r; 1986s;

1986t; Otto 1969; 1991; Dirks 1968; 1983a; 1983b; 1985; 1987; 1988; Metz 1978; 1980; Metz/Habermas/Sölle 1994; Metz/ Peters 1991; Metz/Rendtorf 1971; Metz/Wiesel 1993; Küng 1978; 1990b; 1991a; 1991b; Küng/Ess/Stietencron/Bechert 1984; Küng/Homolka 2009; Küng/Kuschel 1993b; Kuschel 1990; Kuschel/Schlensog 2008; Benedict XVI 2011). Hegel, the believer, did not want to end his dialectical philosophy of religion in that negative way. But he could not help it, that this disharmony between religion and secular enlightenment was present, nevertheless, in the social and historical reality of the Western civilization (Hegel 1986q: 342-344; Dragicevic/Oyen 2009: 66-69, 94-96, 121-132 166-174; Boer 2010: 50-56. Moore 2009; Ferguson 2010; Siebert 2011: 147-171).

The Fall of the Roman Empire

Hegel compared - informed by the historian Gibbons - the European civilization of his time with the late Roman Empire and its fall (Hegel 1986l: 339-412; 1986q: 342-344). In the time of the late Roman empire, so Hegel remembered, the universal unity in religion had disappeared, and the Divine had been profaned, and God was dead, and, furthermore, the general political life was characterized by an extreme lack of advice, council, action, and confidence (Hegel 1986q: 289-292, 342-344; 1986g:339- 397, 398-514; 1986l: 339-412; Vahanian 1967; 1977). Reason had fled exclusively into the form of private or abstract right, including property, contract, and the criminal violations of both, and their punishment (Hegel 1986g:92-202; 1986l:339-412). Because what was objectively in and for itself in state and religion had been given up, the particular physical and psychological well being of the private person, the bourgeois, had been elevated into the main purpose of the public life of civil society as the state of necessity and analytical understanding (Hegel 1986g: 203-291, 339-397; 1986i; 1986j; 1986l: 339-412). In the perspective of the dialectical religiology, as in Greece before, so in Rome civil society destroyed the state (Hegel 1986l: 275-338; 339-542; Buber 1952). Plato had tried to rescue the Athenian state through repressing civil society, but failed (Hegel a: 82; 85, 205, 227, 244, 314, 386; 1986b: 97-98, 228, 234, 243, 318, 372, 422, 485, 492-493, 497, 500, 558; 560; 1986c: 66, 245; Lenin 1972 304-305; Buber 1952; Popper 1968a:1968b; 1969; 1971; Schmidt 2011), Likewise philosophy as well as religion failed in Rome in their attempt to rescue the state from civil society (Hegel 1986g: 203-291, 339-397; 1986l:339-412: Buber 1952; Lortz 1964: 32, 54, 65, 104, 107-108, 127-128, 184, 244, 349, 907, 958; Küng 1994a: 62, 218-219, 222-223, 225, 228, 240-241, 243, 246-248, 255, 258 282, 306, 324, 366, 376, 385-386, 413, 458, 462; Benedict XVI 2011).

The Decline of the West

According to Hegel, in modern civil society and state around 1800, like in the late Roman Empire before, the moral opinion of the individual, his own personal view and conviction without objective truth have made themselves into that, what is alone valid in civil society and constitutional state (Hegel 1986g: 92-202, 293-291; 339-397, 398 - 512; 1986 q: 343-344; Habermas 1962; 1969; 1975; 1976; 1977; 1978a; 1978b; 1978c; 1978d; 1979a; 1979b; 1981a; 1981b; 1983; 1984a; 1984b; 1985a; 1985b; 1986; 1987a; 1987b; 1987c; 1987d; 1988a; 1988b; 1990; 1991; 1991c; 1992a; 1992b; 1992c; 1995; 1997a; 1997b; 1998; 1999; 2001a; 2001c; 2002; 2003b; 2004c; 2006c; 2009; Habermas/Bovenschen 1981; Habermas/Luhmann 1975; Habermas/Ratzinger 2006; Honneth 1985; 1990; 1993; 1994; 1996a; 1996b; 2000; 2001; : 54-63; 2002a; 2004; 2005; 2007; Honneth/Joas 2002; Moore 2009; Ferguson 2010). The mania and addiction of private right, i. e. property and contracts, and of pleasure and consumption, are alone on the agenda and on the order of the day (Hegel 1986g: 92-202, 203-291,

339-397; 1986l: 491-542; 1986q: 343-345; Habermas/Bovenschen 1981; Habermas/Luhmann 1975; Habermas/Ratzinger 2006; Honneth 1985; 1990; 1993; 1994; 1996a; 1996b; 2000; 2001; 54-63; 2002a; 2004; 2005; 2007; Honneth/Joas 2002; Moore 2009; Ferguson 2010). When in modern Western civilization the time - the *Kairos* - was fulfilled, so Hegel argued in almost Biblical terms, so that the justification of facts and events through the dialectical notion was a real need, - and this time was now, the beginning of the 19th century -, then there was no longer present in the immediate consciousness of the people, in the reality of modern civil society. the unity of the internal religious and the external secular world of man, and in this antagonism nothing was justified any longer through religious faith (Hegel 1986g:339-397; 1986q: 343-344; Jung 1933; 1958; 1990; Eliade 1961; Tillich 1926; 1929; 1933; 1948; Fromm 1950; 1959; 1966b; 1970b; 1974; 1976; 1980b; 1992; 1995; 1999; 2001; Habermas 1969; 1970; 1971; 1973; 1976; 1977; 1978c; 1978d; 1982; 1987b; 1987c; 1988a; 1988b; 1991a; 1992b; 1992c; 2001a; 2002; 2004b; 2005; 2006a; 2006b'2007; Habermas/Borenschen 1981; 1974; 1975; 2006; Moore 2009; Ferguson 2010). In Hegel's view, the harshness of an objective command or order, an external insistence, the power of the state could here no longer have any effect. For such measures the antagonism and disharmony between the internal and external world of the individual has become too intense and the decline has penetrated too deeply into the Western civilization (Hegel 1986g:339-397; 1986q: 343-344; Jung 1933; 1958; 1990; Eliade 1961; Tillich 1926; 1929; 1933; 1948; Fromm 1950; 1959; 1966b; 1970b; 1974; 1976; 1980b; 1992; 1995; 1999; 2001; Moore 2009; Ferguson 2010). The theologian Hegel still remembered the *Evangelium*:

You are the salt of the earth. But if salt becomes tasteless, what can make it salty again? It is good for nothing, and can only be thrown out to be trampled under foot by men.

You are the light of the world. A city built on a hilltop cannot be hidden. No one lights a lamp to put it under a tub; they put it on the lamp stand, where it shines for everyone in the house. In the same way your light must shine in the sight of men, so that, seeing your good works, they may give the praise to your Father in Heaven.

(Matthew 5:13-16; Hegel 1986q: 343-344; Thierse 2011: 20-23; Moore 2009; Ferguson 2010). In the present late capitalist society, nothing is justified any longer by faith or dialectical reason, and everything is treated positivistically, and almost everything has been technologized, functionalized, mechanized, robotized, computerized, and commercialized in globalized civil society (Hegel 1986g: 339-397; 1986q 343-344; Benjamin 1950; 1955a; 1955b; 1955c; 1968; 1972; 1974; 1977; 1978a; 1978c; 1978d; 1980; 1983a; 1983b; 1987; 1995b; 1995c; 1996a; 1996c; Adorno 1951; 1952: 585-595; 1962; 1963; 1966; 1969a; 1969b; 1969c; 1969d; 1970a; 1970b; 1973b; 1973d; 1973e; 1974; 1976; 1979; 1980a; 1980b; 1980c; 1991a; 1993b; 1993c; 1994; 1995b; 1996; 1997b; 1997c; 1997d; 1997f; 1997h; 1997i-1; 1997j-1; 1997j-2; 1997u; 1998a; 1998b; 1998c; 1998d; 2000a; 2000c; 2000d; 2001a; 2001b; 2001c; 2002a; 2003b; 2003c; 2003d; 2007; Adorno/Kereenyi 1998; Adorno/Kogon 1958a: 392-402; 1958b: 4848 - 498; Adorno/ Frenkel-Brunswick etc. 1950; Ferguson 2010 Moore 2009), The baptized Catholic Adorno, the friend of the Left-Catholic Walter Dirks, and the other critical theorists Bloch and Fromm, agreed with the Catholic poet Eichendorff, a contemporary of Schelling and Hegel, that the realm of faith - the Medieval City of God - had ended (Augustine 1952; 1958; 1984; Adorno 1997k: 69-74; Scheible1989: 7-20; Fromm 1950; 1957; 1959; 1961; 1964; 1966a; 1966b; 1967; 1968; 1970a; 1970b; 1972a; 1974; 1975; 1976; 1999; 2001; Bloch 1960; 1970; 1970b; 1971a; 1971b; 1972; 1975b; 1975c; 1979; 1985a; 1985b; 1985c; 1985d; 1985e; 2009; Bloc; Reif 1978p; Habermas 1986:1250-126; Siebert 2011b: 25-193).

Love

For Hegel, however, when the *Evangelium* was no longer preached to the poor classes in modern civil society, and when the salt has become tasteless, and when all the religious and metaphysical foundations have silently been removed from bourgeois society, then the people, the proletariat or the precariate, for whose reason, which remains thickset and stocky and undeveloped, the truth could only be present in representations, images, and symbols, could not help any longer the urge, yearning, or longing of their internal world for the totally Other than the external world of the senses with all its injustices (Matthew 5:13-16; Hegel 1986q: 343-344, Tillich 1926; 1929; 1933; 1948; Horkheimer 1936; 1966; 1967a; 1967b; 1970c; 1971; 1972; 1973; 1978; 1981a; 1981b; 1981c; 1985g: chap. 29; 1988a; 1988c; 1988d; 2006; Nida-Rümelin 2011: 23-25; Moore 2009; Ferguson 2010). The simple people of the lower classes still stood closest to the extraordinary, unheard of, infinite love and pain and suffering of the Christ, as they were portrayed in the Evangelium (Matthew 24-28; Mark 13-16; Luke 22 –24l John 13-21; Hegel 1986q:289-292; 343-344; Horkheimer 1974: 96-97; Küng 1970; Moore 2009; Ferguson 2010). However, in secular late bourgeois society this religious love, the Agape, as realization of the universal Golden Rule had been turned and transformed into erotic and sexual love, and pleasure, and consumption (Küng 1990a; 1990b; 1991a; 1991b; 1994a; 2004 Moore 2009; Ferguson 2010; Benedict XVI 2011). Almost forgotten is in secular late capitalist society, determined by money and power, the universal religious commandment:

Love your fellow as yourself

as realization of the Golden Rule (Leviticus 19: 18; Matthew 5:43-48; Küng 1991b; 1994a; 2004; Moore 2009; Ferguson 2010; Benedict XVI 2011). When Rabbi Hillel was once asked by a gentile to summarize the Torah in one sentence, he offered a version of the Golden Rule, present

in all great world religions:
What is distasteful to you, don't do to another person.
The rest is commentary; now go study the commentary

(Leviticus 1918; Lieber 2001:697; Küng 1970; 1978, 1982; 1991a; 1991b; 1994a; 1994b; 2004; 2009; Küng/Ess/ StietencronBechert 1984; Küng. /Homolka 2009; Küng/ Kuschel 1993a; 1993b; Kuschel 1990; Kuschel/Schlensog 2008; Moore 2009; Ferguson 2010; Benedict XVI 2011), Hillel taught more precisely, that people should love their neighbor, because he or she was like them, subject to the same temptations that they were (Leviticus 19: 18; Matthew 5: 43-48; Lieber 2001 697/18), Just as people excuse their own behavior by seeing it in context, claiming that they were tired, angry, or misinformed, and, therefore, guilty of nothing worse than poor judgment, they should be prepared to judge the behavior of others as charitably. Martin Buber understood this commandment as being connected with the preceding one in the book Leviticus:
You shall not take vengeance.
(Leviticus 18: 18; 24:17-22;Matthew 5:38-48; Lieber 2001: 697/18; Buber 1906; 1908; 1913; 1916; 1922; 1923; 1928; 1933; 1935a; 1935b; 1945; 1947; 1948; 1950a; 1950b; 1951; 1952; 1953; 1954; 1958; 1962; 1965). In Buber's view, because all human beings were part of the same body, to hurt another person in an effort to get even, was to hurt part of oneself. Buber compared it to a person, whose hand slips while holding a knife and he stabbed himself. Should, so Buber asked, the person stab the offending hand that slipped to get even with it for hurting him? The person will only hurt himself as second time. So it was, so Buber concluded, when people, in anger, hurt another person, not understanding, that they are all interconnected. According to Buber, anger and a thirst for vengeance corroded the soul. In the perspective of the dialectical religiology, informed

by the Biblical and other world-religions, whenever an individual or a nation did not practice the Golden Rule, the activation of the Lex or Jus Talionis, the law of vengeance, was the iron consequence, as one historical event after the other can prove: World War I, World War II, Fascist Holocaust; Cold War, the Vietnam War, the War of Terror, the Yugoslav Civil War; the War against Afghanistan, the two Iraq Wars, Abu Ghraib, Gutanamo Bay, the Gaza War, the Lebanon War, the Rwanda genocide, the Sudan Civil War, the Libyan War, the cases of Sadam Hussain and of Osama Bin Laden, the global financial crisis of 2008-2011, etc. (Leviticus 18: 18;24: 17-22 Matthew 5:38-48; Lieber 2001: 697/18 Küng 1970; 1978, 1982; 1991a; 1991b; 1994a; 1994b; 2004; 2009; Küng/Ess/StietencronBechert 1984; Küng. /Homolka 2009; Küng/Kuschel 1993a; 1993b; Kuschel 1990; Kuschel/Schlensog 2008; Byrd 2011; Moore 2009; Ferguson 2010; Jacobs 2011: 254-166).The Torah stated:

If anyone kills any human being, he shall be puit to death.One who kills a beast, shall make restitution for it : life for life.If anyone maims his fellow, as he has done so shall it be done to him: fracture for fracture, eye for eye,, tooth for tooth. The injury he inflicted on another shall be inflicted on him.One who kills a beast shall make restitution for it but one who kills a human being shall be put to death. You shall have one standard for stranger and citizen.: for I the Lord am your God.

(Leviticus 24: 17-21; Lieber 2001: 732-733/18)Christianity tried to invert and overcome this *Lex Talionis*.in the Torah. The Sermon on the Mount teaches:

You have learned, how it was said: Eye for eye and tooth for tooth.But I say this to you,offer the wicked man no resistance.Do the contrary, if anyone hits you on the right cheak offer him the other as well; if a man takes you to law and would have your tunic, let him have your cloak as well And if anyone orders you to go one mile, go two miles with him. Give to anyone who asks, and if anyone wants to borrow, do not turn him away.

(Exodus 21: 24; Leviticus 24: 17-21; Matthew 5:38-42)

Judaism, Christianity. Islam

In the perspective of the critical theory of religion, not only the Biblical religions, Judaism as the Religion· of Sublimity, and Christianity as the Religion of Freedom, but also Islam as the Religion of Law, and all the other still living world-religions, were drawn into the always globalizing dichotomy between religious faith and secular bourgeois, Marxian and Freudian enlightenment (Holy Qur'an: Sura I and II; Thomas Aquinas 1922; Hegel 1986q: 336-339; Chardin 1959; Cone 1970; Kolodiejchuk 2007; Berrigan 1972; 1978;1989; Gutierrez 1973;1988;Tillich 1926; 1929; 1933; 1948; 1951; 1952; 1955a; 1955b; 1957; 1963a; 1963b; 1972; 1977; 1983; Cone 1970; Küng 1970; 1978, 1982; 1991a; 1991b; 1994a; 1994b; 2004; 2009; Küng/Ess/Stietencron/Bechert 1984; Küng. /Homolka 2009; Küng/Kuschel 1993a; 1993b; Kuschel 1990; Kuschel/Schlensog 2008; Byrd 2011; Thierse 2011:20-23; Moore 2009; Ferguson 2010; Metz 1959; 1962; 1963; 1965;1967; 1969; 1970; Benedict XVI 2011). According to Hegel, in Islam the human subject was not for himself or for herself against the unity of God, of Allah, into which he or she has emptied out himself or herself (Hegel 1986q: 336-338; Küng 2004). The subject did not retain his or her particularity against this unity of God. The subject gave itself only the determination to immerse himself or herself into the unity of Allah. Thus, the subject has no particular or objective purpose of his or her own, except the honor of the one God. In Islam, there existed an affirmative relationship of the subject to his or her Essence, which is this one God. The subject surrendered himself or herself into this universal unity of God. Islam has the same objective content as the Jewish religion (Hegel 1986q:50-

96; 336-338; Küng 1991b; 2004; Küng / Homolka 2009; Metz/ Wiesel 1993; Benedict XVI 2011). However, in Islam the relationship of man to God has been broadened sociologically. In Judaism and Islam there remained for man no particularity before the unity of God. The Jewish value of nationalism, which was very different from modern nationalism, and which posited the relationship of the subject to the one God, was missing in Islam. There was no national limitation in Islam. In the Religion of Law man behaved as a purely abstract self-consciousness toward the one God. Christianity found in Islam its opposite, because the Muslim religion moved in the same sphere with Christianity (Hegel 1986q:50-96; 336-338; Küng 1991b; 2004; Küng / Homolka 2009; Metz/Wiesel 1993; Byrd 2011; Moore 2009; Ferguson 2010). Islam was like the Jewish religion a spiritual religion of subjectivity, and not a nature religion (Hegel 1986p; 1986q:50-96; 336-338; Küng 1991b; 2004; Küng / Homolka 2009; Metz/Wiesel 1993'Byrd 2011). But only in the abstract, knowing spirit of the human subject Allah was for the self-consciousness and thus stood with the Christian God on the same level, in so far as no particularity is retained. In Islam, whoever feared God was pleasing to Him (Holy Qur'an: Sura I, II, and III; Thomas Aquinas 1922; Hegel 1986q:336-338. ; Byrd 2011). Man has value only insofar has he posited his truth in the knowledge, that the one God was his or her Essence. Islam did not recognize any separation among the believers, or between them and Allah. In Islam, before God the determination of the subjects according to estate, status, rank, or class was superseded. There could *de facto* be estate, rank, status, or class in Islamic countries, but that was considered to be only accidental. And not substantial. There actually existed slavery in Islam (Hegel1986q:336; Küng 2004; Byrd 2011; Moore 2009; Ferguson 2010).

The Messiah

In Hegel's view, the contrast between Christianity and Islam consisted in that in the Rabbi Jesus of Nazareth, called by his friends the Messiah or the Christ, the spirituality was concretely developed, and that it was known as Trinity, i. e. as Spirit concretely superseding in himself Father and Son, and that the history of man, the relationship to the one God, was concrete history, and that it took its beginning from the natural will of man, which was as it ought not to be, and that it was the giving up and surrendering of this natural will: the becoming oneself of man through this negation of himself or herself toward his or her *Essence* (Holy Qur'an: Sura II; Thomas Aquinas 1922; Hegel 1986c; 1986p; 1986q:50-96; 336-338; Tillich 1929; 1933; 1948; 1951; 1952; 1955a; 1955b; Horkheimer 1974:96-97; Küng 1991b; 2004; Küng / Homolka 2009; Metz/Wiesel 1993; Zizek 2007; Zizek/Milbank 2008). In Hegel's view, the Muslim hated and banned everything concrete. God is the absolute One, against whom man retained for himself or herself no purpose, no particularity, and no peculiarity (Hegel 1986q:336-338). However, the really existing human being did admittedly particularize himself or herself in his or her inclinations and interests, and these may even be wilder and more untamed, more uncontrolled, and more unrestrained, because concerning them the analytical reflection of the secular enlightenment was still missing. But then also the very opposite was present in Islam, namely to let everything fall, indifference against any particular purpose, and even against life. (Holy Qur'an: Sura I, II, III; Thomas Aquinas 1922; Hegel 1986p: 203-291; 1986q:336-338; Byrd 2011). No practical purpose was valid as such essentially. As now, however, man was also practical and active, thus there could in Islam the purpose be only, to produce in all human beings the veneration and worshipping of the One, of Allah. Therefore, fanaticism may arise in

Islam. The dialectical religiologist observed such fanaticism at work in Jihadist terror acts in the Near East, Africa, Europe and North America toward the end of the 20th century and at the beginning of the 21st century (Hagerman 2001a; Byrd 2011; Moore 2009; Ferguson 2010). The polemical rebelliousness and revolt of Christianity against that, what ought not to be, in what is the case in society and history reached its climax in the assertion of the believers, that the rich and powerful murderers did ultimately not triumph over the innocent victim, the poor man, Jesus of Nazareth, called the Messiah, the Christ, and his friends under slavery, feudalism and capitalism, throughout the ages (Matthew 26-28; Hegel 1986: 289-306, 306-344; Bloch 1960; 1970a; 1970b; 1971a; 1072b; 1072; 1975b; 1985e; Zizek 2007; 2009; Zizek/ Milbank 2007; Moore 2009; Ferguson 2010).

Enlightenment

For Hegel, the analytical reflection of the bourgeois enlightenment and revolution, and of Jean Jacques Rousseau's and Francois de Voltaire's deism, stood with the Islam on the same theological level: that God had no content and thus was not concrete (Holy Qur'an: Sura II; Thomas Aquinas 1922; Hegel 1986a: 56, 74, 85, 438, 452; 1986b: 420; 1986g: 80, 239, 304, 400; 1986h: 312-313; 1986i: 96, 346 1986j: 278; 1986k: 278; 1986l: 61, 419; 1986o: 352, 370, 414, 503, ; 1986p: 211; 1986q: 337-338; 1986t: 248, 294; Küng 1870; 1972; 1978; 1994a; 1994b; 2004; Moore 2009; Ferguson 2010; Benedict XVI 2011). According to Hegel, that meant that in the bourgeois enlightenment and revolution, like in Islam, there was not present the appearance of God in the flesh, the elevation of Christ into the Son of God, the transfiguration of the finitude of the world and of man's self-consciousness into the infinite self-determination of God (Holy Qur'an: Sura I, . II, III; Thomas Aquinas 1922; Hegel 1986a: 56, 74, 85, 438, 452; 1986b: 420; 1986c; 1986g: 80, 239, 304, 400;

1986h: 312-313; 1986i: 96, 346 1986j: 278; 1986k: 278; 1986l: 61, 419, 520-542; 1986o: 352, 370, 414, 503, ; 1986p: 211; 1986q: 337-338; 1986t: 248, 294 Küng 1870; 1972; 1978; 1994a; 1994b; 2004; Moore 2009; Ferguson 2010; Benedict XVI 2011). For the bourgeois enlighteners, as for Islam before, Christianity meant only a teaching. Christ who was merely a messenger of God, a divine teacher, a teacher like Socrates (Hegel 1986a: 20, 48, 50, 51-53, 56, 74, 92-83, 85, 91, 119, 120, 438, 452; 1986b: 206, 420, 497-498; 1986c; 1986d: 272, 287, 446, 1986g: 80, 239, 304, 400; 1986f: 109, 557, 559; 1986g: 259, 260, 277, 280-281, 282, 303, 448, 1986h: 22, 174, 252, 312-313; 1986i: 96, 346 1986j: 361, 278; 1986k: 226, 255, 256, 278; 300-301, 474; 1986l: 61, 419, 520-542; 1986o: 352, 370, 414, 503 ; 1986p: 211; 1986q: 337-338; 1986t: 248, 294; Küng 1870; 1972; 1978; 1994a; 1994b; 2004; Byrd 2011; Moore 2009; Ferguson 2010). Christ was only more excellent than Socrates, since he was supposedly without sin. For Hegel, the Christology of the modern enlighteners was like that of the Muslims a half-truth: either Christ was only a man, or he was the *Son of Man* (Holy Qur'an: Sura I, . II, III; Thomas Aquinas 1922; Hegel 1986l:520-542; 1986q: 241-298, 337-338; Küng 1970; 1994a; 1994b; 2004; Byrd 2011; Benedict XVI 2011). Thus in the bourgeois enlightenment nothing remained of the concrete divine history, The modern enlighteners sole of Christ as did the Holy Qur'an (The Holy Qur'an: Sura II; Thomas Aquinas 1922; Hegel 1986l:520-542; 1986q:241-298, 337-338; Küng 1970; 1994a; 1994b; 2004; Benedict XVI 2011), . For Hegel, the difference between this stage of bourgeois enlightenment and the Islam consisted only in that the latter, the view of which bathed itself in the ether of the unlimited Infinite, as this abstract independence, gave up everything particular, enjoyment, status, rank, class, private knowledge, and all vanity as such. To the contrary, the standpoint of the bourgeois enlightenment, characterized by analytical understanding, since for its deistic position God was entirely transcendent and had no affirmative relationship toward the human subject, put man abstractly for himself, so that he recognized the affirmative Universal only in so far as it was in himself or herself, but only abstractly. Therefore, the bourgeois enlightener took the fulfilling content of the affirmative Universal out of the factual contingency, accidentality, and arbitrariness of the everyday life world and history (Hegel 1986l:520-542; 1986q:241-298, 337-338; Küng 1970; 1994a; 1994b; 2004; Moore 2009; Ferguson 2010; Benedict XVI 2011).

Reconciliation

Hegel recognized, nevertheless, even in the modern bourgeois deistic enlightenment and revolution a moment of reconciliation (Hegel 1986l: 520-542; 1986q: 338-339; Moore 2009; Ferguson 2010). In this sense, also the deistic enlightenment was a realization of faith in continuation of the declining Christian community. As namely, so Hegel explained, all concrete content of the affirmative Universal had deteriorated and decayed in this enlightened subjectivity, which knew itself in itself infinitely, thereby in it the originally Christian principle of subjective freedom had, nevertheless, become conscious (Hegel 1986l: 520-542; 1986q: 338; Küng 1970; 1984a; 1994b; Benedict XVI 2011; Siebert 1965; 1966; 1978; 1979a; 1979b; 1979c; 1979d; 1979e; 1986; 1987a; 1987b; 1987c; 1987d; 1989; 1993; 1995; 2000; 2001; 2002a; 2005b; 2010b; Moore 2009; Ferguson 2010). That what had been called internality in the Christian community, was now in the revolutionary bourgeois enlightenment movement developed in itself. It was now not only internality, i. e. e. conscience, but it was also the subjectivity, which judged or differentiated itself in itself, and was thus concrete, and which was as its objectivity, which knew the Universal in itself, which it produced out of itself (Hegel 1986g: 203-291; 1986l: 520-542; 1986q: 338-

339; Küng 1978; Benedict XVI 2011). This enlightened subjectivity was for itself. It determined itself in itself. It was the completion of the subjective extreme into the Idea in itself (Hegel 1964; 1986c; 1986f; 1986h; 1986g; 1986t; Küng 1978). For Hegel, the deficiency in this completion of subjective freedom into the Idea was that it was merely formal: bourgeois formalism (Hegel 1964; 1986c; 1986f; 1986h; 1986g; 1986t; Horkheimer 1987b:15-74, 75-148; Küng 1978; Moore 2009; Ferguson 2010). It lacked true objectivity. It was the last peak of the bourgeois formal cultural formation and education, without any necessity in itself. In Hegel's view, it belonged to the true completion of the Idea, that the objectivity was let free: that it be the totality of the objectivity in itself. Thus, the result of this objectivity was that in the subject all was like a bubble, without real objectivity, without firm determination: without the concrete development of the affirmative Universal, of God (Hegel 1964; 1986c; 1986f; 1986h; 1986g; 1986t; Küng 1970; 1972; 1978; 1981a; 1982; 1990a; 1990b; 1991a; 1991b; 1992; 1993a; 1994a; 1994b; 2004; Kuschel/Schlensog 2008; Moore 2009; Ferguson 2010; Benedict XVI 2011). For Hegel, this last peak of the formal cultural formation and education of his time - the bourgeois revolution and enlightenment and restoration- was at the same time the highest rawness, crudeness, and, brute force, because it possessed of the cultural formation and education only the abstract form (Hegel 1986b:123, 314, 465; 465; 1986c: 24, 55, 109, 114; 156; 415, 510;, 1986l: 520-542; 1986q:336-344, 347-535; Horkheimer 1987b: 15-74 75- 148, 149-153; 1987k:13-118; 1985g:: chaps. 1-6, 8, 11, 13, 18; 20; 21; 22; 23; 24; 31; 33; 34; 35; . 36; 37; 38; 39; 40; 41; 43; 1988d: chaps 1; 3; 5; 6; 7; 8; 9; 12; 13; Moore 2009; Ferguson 2010 ; Benedict XVI 2011).

The Extremes

At the end of the 20th century and in the beginning of the

21st century, 200 years after Hegel's death, the dialectical religiologist still observes two extremes having developed in consequence of the decline and desubstantialization of the Christian community particularly in the history of science, and of law, and of journalism, and being in collision with each other in terms of a global culture war:

1. Islam, characterized by the unfreedom of the abstract individual in the absolute region of freedom,
2. The bourgeois enlightenment, characterized by abstract subjectivity and formal subjective freedom without content

(Hegel 1986b: 123, 314, 465; 465; 1986c: 24, 55, 109, 114; 156; 415, 510; 1986l: 520-542; 1986q:336-344, 347-535; Horkheimer 1987b: 15-74 75-148, 149-153; 1987k:13-118; 1985g:: chaps. 1-6, 8, 11, 13, 18; 20; 21; 22; 23; 24; 31; 33; 34; 35; . 36; 37; 38; 39; 40; 41; 43; 1988d: chaps 1; 3; 5-9; 12; 13; Küng 1970; 1978; Moore 2009; Ferguson 2010). Both extremes produced out of their abstractness and formalism revengeful fanatic terrorism and counter-terrorism, without regard for the religious Golden Rule or its secular inversion and translation into the categorical imperative, and later on into the communicative or discourse ethics, determined by the *apriori* of the unlimited communication community (Kant 1929; 1946; 1968; 1970; 1974a; 1974b; 1975; 1981; 1982; 1983; Hegel 1896; 1965; 1969; 1972; 1976; 1979; 1986a; 1986b; 1986c; 1986g; 1986q:338; Horkheimer 1988d: chaps. 1, 3; Greers 1935; Neumann 1942; Apel 1975; 1976a; 1976b; 1982; 1990; Adorno 1951; 1952; 1962; 1963; 1966; 1969a; 1959b; 1969c; 1970a; ; 1970b; 1976; Adorno/Benjamin 1994; Adorno/ Dirks (eds) 1974; Dirks/Kereenyi 1998; Adorno/Kogon 1958a: 342-402; 1958b: 484-498; Adorno-Frenkel-Brunswick, etc. (eds) 1950; Hagerman 1962; 1969; 1970; 1971; 1976; 1977; 1978a; 1978c; 1978d; 1981b; 1983; 1984a; 1984b; 1985a; 1985b; 1986; 1987a; 1988a; 1988b; 1990; 1991a; 1991b; 1991c;

1992a; 1992b; 1992c; 1995; 1997a; 1997b; 1998; 1999; 2001a; 2001c; 2002; 2003b; 2004a; 2004b; 2004c; 2005; 2006a; 2006b; 2006c; 2006d; 2007; 2009; Habermas/Boverschen 1981; Habermas/Henrich 1974; Habermas/Ratzinger 2006; Habermas/Lumann 1975; Honneth 1965; 1990; 1993; 1994; 1996a; 1996b; 2000; 2002a; 2004; 2005; 2007; Honneth/Joas 2002; Moore 2009; Ferguson 2010). The theological abstractness and formalism of Islam lead to religious terror against the Western secular bourgeois and socialist enlightenment movements and revolutions (Hegel 1986q:333-344; Siebert 2010b; Horkheimer 1988d: chaps. 1, 3; Habermas 2001a; Greers 1935; Neumann 1942 Moore 2009; Ferguson 2010), The philosophical abstractness and formalism of the bourgeois enlightenment led to a secular terror of virtue and democracy (Hegel 1986l: 520-542; 1986q:333-344; Horkheimer 1988d: chaps. 1, 3; Habermas 2001a; Greers 1935; Neumann 1942; Moore 2009; Ferguson 2010; Siebert 2010b), The Chinese proverb is right: in its head the fish stinks first (Hegel 1986l:142-173; 1986p:302-330; Moore 2009; Ferguson 2010).

Clashes

In the first decade of the 21st century, the extremes' revengeful clashes and collisions with each other climaxed in the September 11, 2001 catastrophe in New York, in terror and counter-terror attacks in the Near East, Afghanistan, Iraq, Pakistan, Africa, Europe and North America, and in the killing of ten thousands of innocent victims on both sides, and in the hanging of Sadam Hussein, and in the assassination of Osama Bin Laden (Habermas 2001a; 2001c; 2002; 2004b; 2005; 2006a; 2006b; 2006c; 2007; 2009; Huntington 1996; 1998 ; Bin Laden 2005; Byrd 2011; Byrd 2011; Moore 2009; Ferguson 2010;). When the saintly Pope John Paul II warned US President George W. Bush, not to invade Iraq and wage a war against it, he was totally ignored, in spite of the fact that he had strongly supported the neo-liberal counter-revolution of 1989 in Poland, and in Eastern Europe (Mercieca 2011; Moore 2009; Ferguson 2010). The Pope insisted, that such a war would be immoral, and that it might turn the whole region into a quagmire with great animosity developing against Christians, which indeed it did. The born again, neo-liberal President Bush had the support of all the pro-life politicians in invading Iraq for reasons, that later were proven to be entirely false. The infrastructures of several Iraqian cities were destroyed with tens of thousands of innocent people killed brutally and mercilessly, including hundreds of pregnant women, Two million people became refugees, having lost their homes and all of their belongings. More than three quarters of a million children became orphans, many of whom lost the will to live, which may explain the story of the Islamic suicide bombers at least to some extend. As a result of the war, numerous Iraqi children were born deformed. When leading American neo-liberal, so called pro-life politicians were asked as to the number of Iraqi people that lost their lives following the US invasion, their quick answer was:

We do not keep account of such incidents, since we consider this merely as collateral damage.

(Mercieca 2011; Moore 2009; Ferguson 2010). Obviously, the US self-proclaimed pro-life politicians view quite inconsistently the loss of the lives of Iraqis or -for that matter - Afghanis, or Pakistanis, or Lebanese, or Libyans, or Palestinians, etc. not as a sacred element, but just as a *thing*: a piece of furniture (Fromm 1950; 1956; 1957; 1959; 1961; 1967; 1970a; 1970b; 1972; 1973; 1974; 1975; 1976; 1980b; 1981; 1990a; 1990b; 1995; 1997; 1999;, 2001; Fromm/Suzuki/ Martino 1960; Fromm/Xirau 1979; Mercieca 2011; Byrd 2011; Moore 2009; Ferguson 2010).

Idolatry

In the American civil society, the continued manufacture and sales of weapons, along with the waging of wars, have turned into a great lucrative business for what President Eisenhower has called the Military-Industrial-Congressional Complex. (Fromm 1950; 1956; 1957; 1959; 1961; 1967; 1970a; 1970b; 1972; 1973; 1974; 1975; 1976; 1980b; 1981; 1990a; 1990b; 1995; 1997; 1999;, 2001; Fromm/Suzuki/Martino 1960; Fromm/Xirau 1979; Mercieca 2011; Moore 2009; Ferguson 2010; Benedict XVI 2011), As a monopoly-oligopoly- capitalist country, the USA views money and wealth and power as its god. For this idolatry of capital anything is allowed to take place: even the vicious breaking of the Mosaic *Ten Commandments*, which all three Abrahamic Religions have in common, and which include among other rules, *you should not steal or destroy the property of others*; *you should not kill*; and *you should not tell lies* (Exodus 20; Psalm 106;Fromm 1966; Mercieca 2011; Moore 2009; Ferguson 2010), When the Rabbi Jesus of Nazareth was asked, who he was, there was only one answer that he gave: *I am the Way, the Truth, and the Life* (John 14:16; Mercieca 2011; Benedict XVI 2011). In the perspective of the dialectical religiology, confronted with this Biblical reality it is incomprehensive for US clergymen to formulate the slogan: *If you are for-life, you vote pro-life.* If a US politician is *pro-life and pro-peace* at the same time, then considering voting for such an individual would be appropriate. But if such a politician proves to be *pro-life* and *pro-war* at the same time, then voting for such an individual should be totally out of the question. The idolatry of the maximalization of profit and power is the source of all other sins in private and public life. Under the guise of *national defense and security* self-proclaimed pro-life. politicians in particular and the clergy, who support them, believe, that they can do anything, that crosses their minds (Adorno 1997i-1:7-142, 149-509; Mercieca 2011; Benedict

XVI 2011; Moore 2009; Ferguson 2010). The old Romans used to say : *Si vis pacem, para pacem,* or *Si vis bellum, para bellum.* (Hegel 1986l: 339-542; Mercieca 2011). The neo-conservative US President Richard Nixon invented the new slogan: *If you want peace, prepare for war,* and thus outdid the Romans (Hegel 1986l:107-114; 339- 412; Mercieca 2011; Moore 2009; Ferguson 2010).

Wars

There was a time, when the Church spoke of justifiable wars in terms of the *Augustinian Seven Point Just War Theory,* and, as a result, initiated crusades to kill Moslems, to prevent them from taking hold of the holy places in Jerusalem and Palestine,and blessed both hostile armies and their murder weappns through the centuries up to Hiroschima amd Nagasaki(Lortz 1962: 309, 323, 327, 328-330, 331-332, 333, 336, 352, 376, 380, 389, 401, 403, 405, 423, 425, 435, 437-439, 800, 946; Küng 1994a:: 184 194, 200, 206-209, 210-211. 215-217, 219, 687, 711, 743; Mercieca 2011; Byrd 2011; Moore 2009; Ferguson 2010; Baron 2011: 65-68;Kesting 2011:68-70;Hochgeschwender 2010;Keegan 2010; MacPherson 2010-). A thousand years later, Pope John Paul II apologized with tears in his eyes, asking God and the world for forgiveness for the needless massacre of so many innocent lives in Palestine, in the Holy Land: Moslems as well as Jews. A couple of years later his successor, the German Pope Benedict XVI, stated emphatically:

war is never justified under any circumstance whatsoever

(Pope John XXIII 1962; Mercieca 2011; Tierse 2011: 20-23; Moore 2009; Ferguson 2010; Baron 2011: 65-68;Kesting 2011:68-70;Hochgeschwender 2010;Keegan 2010; MacPherson 2010). While so called pro-choice politicians do not really do anything to force women into having an abortion, pro-life politicians and their clerical supporters continue most inconsistently and irrationally to provide all the lethal means for people to annihilate each other. While pro-choice politicians may be co-responsible for the killing of the unborn, only one at a time, amounting admittedly to a million a year in the American society alone, neo-liberal pro-life politicians and supportive clergy are co-responsible for the continued waging of wars and for the brutal massacre of tens of thousands of pregnant women and their babies at a time, amounting to millions on a global scale. While for pro-life politicians it is unethical, and immoral, and criminal to kill the unborn, it is fully alright to kill mercilessly and brutally the unborn baby with the mother as well, which happens each time all kinds of most sophisticated weapons are used to bombard and destroy hospitals, schools, and residences, where civilians, non-combatants, live. In the perspective of the dialectical religiology, informed by Biblical religion and humanism, it would be wise for clergymen and -women, in their justified defense of life to condemn very strongly out of Biblical and humanistic reasons the continued manufacture and sales of weapons and the continued waging of more struggles and wars, may it be in Iraq, Afghanistan, Pakistan, Palestine, Lebanon, Libya, or elsewhere (Mercieca 2011; Byrd 2011; Moore 2009; Ferguson 2010;Baron 2011:65-68;Kesting 2011:68-70;Hochgeschwender 2010;Keegan 2010; MacPherson 2010-Siebert 1965; 2010b) . In the USA, unfortunately, these destructive war elements and the idolatry and apostasy of the *Golden Calf,* which they feed, are viewed as the *Holy Cow,* that as an idol, has become increasingly difficult to criticize on Biblical or humanistic grounds, and to take realistic steps to help to reverse this destructive trend (Exodus 32; Horkheimer 1988d: chaps 1, 2, 3, 6, 7 11; Fromm 1950; 1956; 1957; 1959; 1961; 1966c; 1967; 1970a; 1970b; 1972; 1973; 1974; 1975; 1976; 1980b; 1981; 1990a; 1990b; 1995; 1997; 1999; Fromm/Suzuki/Martino 1960; Fromm/Xirau 1979; Mercieca 2011; Moore 2009; Ferguson 2010; Baron 2011: 65-

68;Kesting 2011:68-70;Hochgeschwender 2010;Keegan 2010; MacPherson 2010;' Siebert 1965; 2010b).

Future

In the perspective of the critical theory of society and religion, in the future both extremes must be transcended through their mediation (Hegel 1896; 1965; 1969; 1972; 1976; 1979, 1986a; 1986b; 1986c; 1986g; 1986q:338; Apel 1975; 1976a; 1976b; 1982; 1990; Adorno 1951; 1952; 1962; 1963; 1966; 1969a; 1959b; 1969c; 1970a; 1970b; 1976; Habermas 2001a; 2001c; 2002; 2004b; 2005; 2006a; 2006b; 2006c; 2007; 2009; Neiman 2011: 48-51; Maas 2011: 48-51; Moore 2009; Ferguson 2010; Baron 2011: 65-68; Kesting 2011:68-70;Hochgeschwender 2010;Keegan 2010; MacPherson 2010). The human subjectivity must develop out of itself the concrete content of the *Affirmative Universal; the Good Infinity; the Idea greater than which nothing can be thought, and which, therefore, also contains being and is; Heaven; Eternity; Beauty; . Truth;, the Eternal One; the Ultimate Reality; the X-Experience; the Entirely Non-Identical, the Absolutely New; the. Totally Other.* (Anselm 1962; Blakney 1941; Kant 1929; 1946; 1968; 1970; 1974a; 1974b; 175; 1981; 1982; 1983; Hegel 1896; 1964; 1965; 1969; 1972; 1976; 1979, 1986a; 1986b; 1986c; 1986e; 1986g; 1986h; 1986l; 1986q:338, 347-536; Apel 1975; 1976a; 1976b; 1982; 1990; . Horkheimer 1936; 1966; 1967a; 1967b; 1970c; 1971; 1972; 1973; 1974a; 1974b; 1974c; 1978; 1981a; 1981b; 1981c; 1985g: chaps 17, 23, 25, 26, 27, 28, 29, 30, 32, 34, 37, 49; 1987c; 1988a; 1991f; 2006; Benjamin 1950; 1955a; 1955c; 1968; 1972; 1974; 1977; 1978a; 1978b; 1978e; 1978d; 1980; 1983a; 1983b; 1995b; 1995c; 1996a; 1996b; 1996c; 1997; Fromm 1932a; 1932b; 1950; 1956; 1957; 1959; 1961; 1964; 1966a: 57-58; 1966b; 1967; 1968; 1970a; 1970b; 1972a; 1972b; 1973; 1974; 1976; 1980b; 1981; 1990a; 1990b; 1992; 1995; 1997; 1999:: 34-36; 2001; Reich 1971; 1976; Marcuse 1970a: chap 1; Adorno 1951; 1952; 1962; 1963; 1966; 1969a; 1959b; 1969c; 1970a; ; 1970b;

1976; Adorno/Benjamin 1994; Adorno/Dirks (eds) 1974; Dirks/Kereenyi 1998; Adorno/Kogon 1958a: 342-402; 1958b: 484-498; Adorno-Frenkel-Brunswick, etc. (eds), 1950; Habermas 1962; 1969; 1970; 1971; 1976; 1977; 1978a; 1978c; 1978d; 1981b; 1983; 1984a; 1984b; 1985a; 1985b; 1986; 1987a; 1988a; 1988b; 1990; 1991a; 1991b; 1991c; 1992a; 1992b; 1992c; 1995; 1997a; 1997b; 1998; 1999; 2001a; 2001c; 2002; 2003b; 2004a; 2004b; 2004c; 2005; 2006a; 2006b; 2006c; 2006d; 2007; 2009; Habermas/Boverschen 1981; Habermas/Henrich 1974; Habermas/Ratzinger 2006; Habermas/Luhmann 1975; Honneth 1965; 1990; 1993; 1994; 1996a; 1996b; 2000; 2002a; 2004; 2005; 2007; Honneth/Joas 2002; Schmidt 2011; Kuschel/Schlensog 2008; Moore 2009; Ferguson 2010). But this Affirmative Universal must be thought of according to an internal necessity: that the human subject knows and recognizes this concrete content as necessary and as objective in and for itself. That precisely is the standpoint of the critical theory of society and religion, that the theological content takes flight into the dialectical notion, and that it receives through thinking and acting, through theory and praxis, its restoration and justification possibly in the form of a naturalistic-humanistic, not authoritarian, post-theistic mystical religiosity: i. e. in a materialistic, concrete super session of Hegel's logic as Logos-theology and theodicy, which was originally rooted in the mystical theology of Master Eckhart and of Jacob Boehme, and which supposedly contained in itself all the categories, which God thought before he created nature, and man, as the source of history (Genesis I, II; John I; Hegel 1964; 1965; 1969; 1976; 1979; 1986a; 1986b; 1986c; 1986e; 1986f; 1986g; 1986h; 1986l; 1986p; 1986q: 338-339, 347-546; Tillich 1926; 1924; 1933; 1948; 1951; 1952; 1955a; 1950b; Fromm 1966:54-58; 2001; Habermas 1973; 1975; 1976; 1977; 1978a; 1978c; 1978d; 1979a; 1979b; 1981b; 1982; 1983; 1984a; 1984b; 1085a; 1985b; 1985; 1987b; 1987c; 1987d; 1988a; 1988b; 1991a; 1991b; 1991c; 1992a; 1992b; 1992c;

1997a; 1997b; 1999; 2001a; 2001b; 2001c; 2002; 2003a; 2003c; 2004a; 2004b; 2004c; 2005; 2006a; 2006b; 2006d; 2007; Habermas/ Henrich 1974; Habermas/ Ratzinger 2006; Kuschel/Schlensog 2008; Moore 2009; Ferguson 2010; Siebert 2010b). This new, post-theistic mystical Logos - theology would not start, like that of Hegel, with the categories of Being, Nothing and Becoming, but rather with the notions of Something, Infinite and Finite (Hegel 1896; 1964; 1986c; 1986e; 1986f; 1986h; Buber 1962; Adorno 1963; 1966; 1969a; 1969b; 1969c; 1970b; 1973b; 1974; 1982; 1990; 1997a; 1997b; 1997c; 1997e; 1997f; 1998a; 1998b; 1998c; 1998d; 2000e; 2001c; 2002a; 2002d; 2003b; 2003d; Adorno/Kogon 1958a: 392-402; 1958b: 484-498; Horkheimer 1936; 1966; 1967a; 1967b; 1980a; 1970c; 1971; 1972; 1973; 1974a; Habermas 1969; 1970; 1971; 1973; 1971; 1973; 1976; 1977; 1978a; 1978c; 1978d; 1984a; 1988a; 1988b; 1991a:Part III; 1992c; 1997a; 1999; ; 2001a; 2002; 2001b; 2001c; 2994b; 2004c; 2005; 2006a; 2006b; 2006d; 2007; Habermas/Henrich 1974; Habermas/Ratzinger 2006; Kuschel/Schlensog 2008; Moore 2009; Ferguson 2010; Siebert 2009b).

Working-class

According to the dialectical religiology, as in the 19th, 20th and 21st centuries the modern antagonism between the religious and the secular went deeper and deeper in civil and later in socialist society, particularly the fourth estate, the proletariat, the precariate, the working-class felt more and more abandoned by their teachers, intellectuals, and theologians (Hegel 1986q:342-344; Thierse 2011:20-23; Nida-Rümelin 2011: 23-25; Moore 2009; Ferguson 2010; Baron 2011: 65-68;Kesting 2011:68-70;Hochgeschwender 2010;Keegan 2010; MacPherson 2010). In Hegel's view, these teachers had admittedly helped themselves through reflection and enlightenment. They had found their satisfaction in finitude, in subjectivity and its virtuosity, and precisely thereby in vanity. But in such vanity the substantial core of the people could not find its own satisfaction. For the dialectical philosophers, the philosophical knowledge had resolved the dissonance, disharmony and contradiction between the sacred and the profane in modern civil society. It had been the very purpose of Hegel's philosophy of religion. and critical dialectical philosophy in general, to reconcile reason with the world-religions, and to solve even the otherwise unsolvable theodicy problem: philosophy as theology was the true theodicy (Leibniz 1996; Hegel 1986l:28, 540; 1986p: 88; 1986q; 1986s:497; 1986t: 248; 455; Metz 1959; 1963; 1965; 1967; 1970; 1972a; 1972b; 1973a; 1975b; 1977; 1978; 1980; 1981; 1984; 1995; 1997; 1998; Metz/Habermas/Sölle etc. 1994; Metz/Peters 1991; Metz/Rendtorf (eds) 1971; Metz/Wiesel 1993; Küng 1991b:726-730; Kuschel/Schlensog 2008; Oelmüller 1990; 1992; Moore 2009; Ferguson 2010; Baron 2011: 65-68;Kesting 2011:68-70;Hochgeschwender 2010;Keegan 2010; MacPherson 2010). It had been the purpose of Hegel's philosophy of religion, to recognize the evolution of religion and its many forms and paradigms as being internally necessary, and to discover in the revealed, or manifest, or Biblical, or absolute religion, in Christianity, the Truth and the Idea (Genesis I, II; John I; Hegel 1896; 1964; 1965; 1969; 1986a; 1986c; 1986f; 1986j; 1986l; 1986p; 1986q: 343-344, 347-536; 1986r; 1986s; 1986t; Küng 1970; 1978, 1982; 1991a; 1991b; 1994a; 1994b; 2004; 2009; Küng/Ess/Stietencron/Bechert 1984; Küng /Homolka 2009; Küng/Kuschel 1993a; 1993b; Kuschel 1990; Kuschel/Schlensog 2008; Moore 2009; Ferguson 2010). However, Hegel had to admit, that this reconciliation between religion and dialectical reason had only been a partial one without an external. i. e. sociological universality (Marcuse 1960; 1961; 1962; 1967; 1967; 1969a; 1969b; 1970a; 1970b; 1973; 1975; 1979; 1980a; 1980b; 1984; 1987; 1995; 2001; 2005; Moore 2009; Ferguson 2010). For Hegel, in this respect the dialectical philosophy was a separate sanctuary, and its servants constituted an isolated priesthood, which was not allowed to go together and to cooperate with the world, with modern civil society, and which had to guard the possession of the Truth. In Hegel's view, how the temporal, empirical present, i. e., the bourgeois society, the third and fourth estate, the bourgeoisie and the proletariat, would find their way out of the continually deepening antagonism between the sacred and the profane, and how this present would form itself throughout all its culture wars, had to be left to it. It was not the immediate practical issue and task of the dialectical philosophy as theology and theodicy (Hegel 1986q: 343-344, 347-536; 1986r; 1986s; 1986t; Oelmüller 1990; 1992; Küng 1970; 1978, 1982; 1991a; 1991b; 1994a; 1994b; 2004; 2009; Küng/Ess/ Stietencron/Bechert 1984; Küng /Homolka 2009; Küng/ Kuschel 1993a; 1993b; Kuschel 1990; Kuschel/Schlensog 2008; Moore 2009; Ferguson 2010). In the perspective of the dialectical religiology, Hegel's greatest student, Marx, tried to take care of this deficiency in his teacher's philosophy in his historical materialism with the help of Feuerbach (Feuerbach 1904; 1957; 1996; Marx 1871; 1906; 1951; 1963; 1956; 1961a; 1961b; 1961c; 1963; 1974; 1974; 1977; 2000; Marx/ Engels 2005). In spite of all the deficiencies intrinsic in Hegel's philosophy, e. g. his theory of war used by the National Socialists and the Fascists, the critical religiologist can still *see land* with him, as once the ancient Israelites after their liberation from Egyptian slavery saw after their journey through the wilderness the new land flowing with milk and honey, or as Hegel once saw land with Heracleitos, whose dialectical logos-philosophy of becoming he took completely into his own *Logic*, which guided him to his anticipation of the Post-European, Post-Modern alternative Future III - a new American and/or Slavic world, characterized by the reconciliation of the particular and the universal, personal autonomy and universal solidarity

(Exodus 40; Ezekiel 20: 4-6; Lieber 2001: 569-572, 712-716; Hegel 1986e: 84; 185, 226; 1986h: 57, 193; 1986i: 146, 336 522; 1986q: 499; 1986r:14, 194, 215; 238; 301, 319-343; Horkheimer 1987b: 336; Neumann 1942; Flechtheim 1971; Moore 2009; Ferguson 2010; Siebert 2010).

Utopia

The critical theorist Adorno remembered the concrete *utopia* - not utopism - of Hegel's contemporary Eichendorff: the *utopia* of the imageless and nameless totally Other (Adorno 1997k:77-78; Horkheimer1996s: 62-67; Horkheimer/Adorno 2002). According to Adorno's student Habermas, wherever this concrete utopia appears, whether in the Hebrew Bible or in the New Testament, in Master Eckhart's or in Jacob Boehme's mystical theology, or in Schelling's *Ages of the World*, or in the young Hegel, or in Adorno, when he quoted and interpreted Eichendorff, it was always connected with ideas of the sphere of relations with others, and with experiences of undisturbed intersubjectivity, of communicative praxis, of felicitous interaction, of reciprocity and distance, of separation and of successful, unspoiled nearness, of vulnerability and complementary caution (Isaiah 60-66; Matthew 5-7; Luke 6; Acts 2: 42-47; 4: 32-37; Blakney 1941; Boehme 1938; 1962; 2005; Hegel 1972; 1976; 1979; 1986a; 1986b; 1986cl; Adorno 1997k:77-78; Horkheimer 1936; 1966; 1967a; 1971; 1972; 1973; 1981c; 1985g: chaps 17; 29; 37; 40; 1988a; 1987k; : 289- 328;, 329- 332; 1996s: 62-67; Horkheimer/Adorno 2002; Habermas 1962; 1969; 1970; 1971; 1976a; 1977; 1978a; 1978c; 1978d; 1983; 1984a:; 1984b; 1986: 125-126; 1987b; 1987d; 1988b; 1991a; 1991b; 1992a; 1992c; 1997a; 1997b; 2001a; 2004b; 2005; 2006b; Siebert 2010b). In Habermas' view, these social ideas and experiences were more fragile than anything that history up till now - 2011- had ever brought forth in the way of structures of communication: an ever more dense and finely woven web of intersubjective relations, that nevertheless made possible a relation between freedom and solidarity, that could only be imagined with interactive models, if at all (Habermas 1962; 1969; 1970; 1971; 1976a; 1977; 1978a; 1978c; 1978d; 1983; 1984a:; 1984b; 1986: 125-126; 1987b; 1987d; 1988b; 1991a; 1991b; 1992a; 1992c; 1997a; 1997b; 2001a; 2004b; 2005; 2006b; Siebert 2010b).

Limitless Fulfillment

According to Adorno, Echendorff had written in one of his poems the utopian verse:

It speaks intoxicatedly the distance/
As of future, great happiness.

(Hegel 1986o: 415- 473; Adorno 1997k:77-78). The conservative Catholic Eichendorff did not speak of the past happiness. So unreliable was already his Catholic conservativism at the time of Hegel and Schelling. . But Eichendorff's *utopia* was a wandering, roaming erotic one. As the heroes of his prose swayed among images of women, which played into each other and which were never contrasted against each other, so Eichendorff's lyrics showed itself seldom bound to the concrete image of one particular sweetheart. In Adorno's view, for Eichendorff any devotion to any particular or single beauty would already have been a betrayal of the universal idea of limitless fulfillment in the totally Other (Adorno 1997k: 77-78; Horkheimer 1985g:chaps 17; 29; 37; 40). Even in Eichendorff's poem

Above the garden through the air,

one of the most enthusiastic and passionate love poems of the German language, neither the sweetheart appeared, nor did the poet talk about himself in relation to her. Only the rejoicing and the merriment were expressed:

She is yours, she is yours!

In Adorno's view, in his love poem Eichendorff put on

name and fulfillment an image- prohibition in the Mosaic and the Kantian sense (Exodus 20; Kant 1929; 1946; 1968; 1970; 1974a; 1974b; 1975; 1981; 1982; 1985; Adorno 1997k:77-78; Horkheimer 1996s: 62-67: Horkheimer/Adorno 2002), After the death of my German Catholic friend Edmund Bolz, a great teacher and for many years a prisoner of war in the Soviet Union, on May 19, 2011, his children Annette,, Judith and Eva-Maria quoted on his memorial card very much in the spirit of Eichendorff and Adorno, Psalm 18:

You lead me out into the distance
You make bright my darkness,

and confessed:
Praemissus non Amissus
(Gone away, but not passed away-
Sent ahead, but not lost).

Hidden and Sublimated Sexuality

Adorno remembered, that the open and unconcealed representation of sexuality was foreign to the older tradition of the German, but not of the French poetry (Hegel 1986o: 415- 473; Adorno 1997k:77-78; Horkheimer 1996s: 62-67: Horkheimer/Adorno 2002), The German poetry on its middle level had to do penance, and atone, and pay dearly for this keeping secret of sexuality from the people with prudishness and a stagnant, low bourgeois shopkeeper idealism. However, for Adorno in the greatest representatives of German poetry this keeping secret of sexuality turned into a blessing. The power of the unspoken, hidden, concretely superseded, sublimated sexuality penetrated into the word, and gave it its sweetness (Schopenhaur 1946; 1977; 1989; Freud 1939; 1946; 1955; 1962a; 1962b; 1964; 1969; 1977; 1992; 1993; 1995a; 1995b Adorno 1997k:77-78). Even still the non-sensual, or non-sensuous, and abstract became with Eichendorff a parable for a formless, totally Other: archaic inheritance or heritage; earlier than the form and at the same time late Transcendence; and the Unconditional beyond the finite shape and figure (Blakney 1941; Schopenhauer 1946; 1977; 1989; Freud 1939; 1946; 1955; 1962a; 1962b; 1964; 1969; 1977; 1992; 1993; 1995a; 1995b; Adorno 1997k: 77-78; Horkheimer 1985g: chaps 17; 29; 37; 40). Eichendorff's most sensuous poem remained in the nightly Invisible:

Above treetops and crops
Into the splendor –
Who can guess?.

Eiehendorff, still being a contemporary of Schelling and Hegel, groped, touched, pressed, and felt his way to the line in Charles Baudelaires *Fleurs du mal:*

O toi qui la nuit rend si belle:

(Baudelaire 1982; Benjamin 1974; 1983a: 301-489; Adorno 1997k:77-78; Horkheimer 1985g: chaps 17; 29; 37; 40). According to Adorno, Eichendorff's aroused romanticism led unconsciously to the threshold of modern literature, and music, and art in general: with its anti-conservative cancellation of power, rule, master and mistress, ladies and gentlemen, and particularly of the domination of one's own Ego over the soul (Hegel 1986c; 1986j; 1986m; 1986n; 1986o; Schopenhauer 1946; 1977; 1989; Freud 1939; 1946; 1955; 1962a; 1962b; 1964; 1969; 1977; 1992; 1993; 1995a; 1995b; Fromm 1932a; 1932b; 1950; 1956; 1959; 1966a; 1966b; 1967; 1968; 1970b; 1972a; 1974; 1976; 1980b; 1981; 1990a; 1990b; 1992; 1995; 1997; 1999; 2001; Fromm (ed) 1966c; Fromm/Suzuki/Martino 1960; Fromm/ Xirau 1979; Baudelaire 1982; Benjamin 1974; 1983a::301-489; Adorno 1932: 356-378; 1951; 1960; 1962; 1963; 1966; 1969a; 1970b; 1973a; 1973b; 1973c; 1980b; 1981; 1997k: 77-78; Horkheimer 1985g: chaps 17; 29; 37; 40; Siebert 1910b).

III. Critique of Religion

From Hegel's death in 1831, throughout the 19th and 20th centuries into the 21st century all European states produced continually more and more scientific advances as well as laws concerning marriage and family, including divorce, abortion, gays and lesbians, stem cell research, eugenics, euthanasia, etc, and economy and polity and international relations, which contradicted the interpretation of reality and orientation of action of the Biblical as well as the other world-religions, and made especially Christianity less and less *substantial* in the Hegelian sense, and thus lead to more and more secularization, and even to the rejection of theism and the construction of a new Atheism in America and Europe. (Hegel 1986c; 1986g: 24 27, 42-43; 1986l: 11-141; 1986q; Feuerbach 1904; 1957; 1996; Marx 1953: 207; Lefebvre1982; Horkheimer 1972: chaps. 1-6, 7; Marcuse 1960; 1961; 1962; 1965; 1967; 1969a; 1969b; 1987; 2001; 2005; Adorno 1997k: 69-74; Fromm 1950; 1957; 1959; 1961; 1964; 1966a; 1966b; 1967; 1968; 1970a; 1970b; 1972a; 1974; 1975; 1976; 1999; 2001; Bloch 1960; 1970; 1970b; 1971a; 1971b; 1972; 1975b; 1975c; 1979; 1985a; 1985b; 1985c; 1985d; 1985e; 2009; Bloc; Reif 1978p; Habermas 1962; 1969; 1970; 1971; 1973, 1976; 1977; 1978a; 1978c; 2001a; 2001c; 2002 Küng 1970; 1978; Thierse 2011: 20-23; Moore 2009; Ferguson 2010; Smith 2011:215-238; Siebert 2011b:: 25-193), In 1844/1845 Hegel's most outstanding disciple and critic, Marx, declared somewhat prematurely in his *On the Critique of the Hegelian Philosophy of Law* of 1843/1844 and in his *Economic-philosophical Manuscripts of 1844*, that he considered the critique of religion essentially completed, at least as far as Germany was concerned (Hegel 1986g; 1986p; 1986q; Marx 1953: 207; Horkheimer 1972: chaps 1-6, 7; 1985l: 286-287; 349- 387, 398- 416, 436- 492, 493- 523, 524- 525, 526- 558, 593- 605; Moore 2009; Ferguson 2010). For Marx, guided by Feuerbach, the critique of religion was the presupposition of all other economic, or political, or cultural critique (Feuerbach 1904; 1957; 1996; Hegel 1986g; Marx 1953: 207; Moore 2009; Ferguson 2010). . In Marx's secular naturalistic-humanistic view, the profane existence of familial, social, economic, political, or cultural error was compromised after its heavenly *Oratio pro aris et focis* had been refuted. Man, who in the imaginary or fantastic religious reality of heaven, where he supposedly searched for a super-man, had found merely the reflection of himself, will no longer be inclined, merely to find the appearance of himself, the non-human, where he searched and must search for his true reality. In the perspective of the dialectical religiology, it must not be forgotten, that the religion, which Marx had before his eyes and which he criticized in Germany, France, Belgium and England, was mainly bourgeoisie religion, the music of which he liked, because it reminded him, that there was once a poor man, Jesus of Nazareth, whom the rich and powerful classes murdered, and let him ask the dominant European and American bourgeoisie in utter indignation: why do you make a liar out of him with every word you say, and with every deed you do? (Marx 1953; Horkheimer 1974: 16, 28, 19-20, 28-29, 38-39, 45, 49; 54, 56, 59-60, 61, 62, 65, 68-69, 71, 75-76, 88, 89, 91-92; 95-96; 92-93, 94-95, 96-97, 98; 99-100, 101-104; Metz 1970; 1972a; 1972b; 1973a; 1973b; 1973c; 1975b; 1977; 1980; 1981; Siebert 1870; 1972a; 1972b; 1973a; 1973b; 1973c; 1975b; 1977; 1980; 1981; 2010b; Moore 2009; Ferguson 2010). In the perspective of the critical theory of society and religion, while for Marx the religious side was first of all the ideological cover-up for the secular side and its antagonisms, e. g. that between labor and capital, the religious side could also contain the power of truth to uncover, what should not be in what was the case on the secular side, and to overcome it (Marx 2000; Baum 1959; 1967; 1968; 1971; 1972; 1975a; 1975b; 1980a; 1980b; 1982; 1991; 1994; 1996; 2001; 2002; 2003; 2004; 2005; 2007; 2009;

Baum (ed) 1999; Gutierrez 1973; 1988; Haag 1981; 1982; 1983; 2005; Moore 2009; Ferguson 2010). The religious side could produce the concrete utopias, by which the secular side could be judged and changed, e. g. the oldest religious utopia of the *land flowing with milk and honey*, where the Hebrew slaves, liberated from their Egyptian masters, were to go (Exodus 7-19, 40; Leviticus 29: 24; Lieber 2001: 703/ 24; More 1895; 1901; 1963; Bloch 1960; 1970a; 1970b; 1971a; 1971b; 1972; 1975a; 1975b; 1975c; 1979; 1985a; 1985b; 1985c; 1985d; 1985e; 2009; Bloch/Reif 1978; Niebuhr 1932; 1964; Moore 2009; Ferguson 2010). There was for Hegel and Marx not only the dialectic between the sacred and the profane, but also the dialectic of the secular and the dialectic of the religious. (Hegel 1986g; 1986p; 1986q; Marx 1953:chaps V, VI; 2000; Horkheimer/Adorno 1969a; 1969b; 1972a; 1972b; 1984; 2002; Moore 2009; Ferguson 2010).

Foundation

According to Marx, the foundation of the radical *(radix-* root, non-religious, humanistic-naturalistic critique was: *Man makes the religion, the religion does not make man* (Hegel 1986g; 1986p; 1986q; Feuerbach 1904; 1957; 1996; Marx 1953: 207; Lefebvre1982; Horkheimer 1972: chaps 1-6, 7; Küng 1970; 1978; Moore 2009; Ferguson 2010). For Marx, religion was the self-consciousness and self-feeling of a man, who had either not yet acquired himself, or who had already lost himself again (Hegel 1986c; 1986g; Feuerbach 1904; 1957; 1996; Marx 1953: 207; Horkheimer 1972: chaps 1-6, 7; Küng 1970; 1978; Moore 2009; Ferguson 2010). However, in Marx's view, the man was not an abstract being, who was squatting or crouching outside the real empirical world. The man was rather the world of man, i. e. the society and the state (Hegel 1986c; 1986g; Feuerbach 1904; 1957; 1996; Marx 1953: 207; Habermas 1969; 1970; 1973; 1976; 1977; 1978a; 1978e; 1978d; 1984a; 1986; 1978b; 1988a; 1990; 1992a; Küng 1970;

1978; Moore 2009; Ferguson 2010). This antagonistic civil society and constitutional state produced the religion, an inverted wrong consciousness of the world, because the world is wrong: it is as it ought not to be. The religion is the universal theory of this wrong world, its encyclopedic compendium, its logic in popular form, its spiritualistic *Point-d'honneur*, its enthusiasm, its moral sanction, its solemn completion and supplement, its general ground of consolation and justification. Religion is the fantastic realization of the human being, because he or she does not have a true reality in the bourgeois as before in the feudal, or slaveholder world (Hegel 1986c; 1986g; 1986p; 1986q; Feuerbach 1904; 1957; 1996; Marx 1953: 207; Marx/Engels 1955; 1960; 2005; Horkheimer 1972:chap 4; Habermas 1969; 1970; 1973; 1976; 1977; 1978a; 1978e; 1978d; 1984a; 1986; 1978b; 1988a; 1990; 1992a; Küng 1970; 1978; Moore 2009; Ferguson 2010). For Marx, the struggle against religion was thus indirectly the struggle against that wrong world, the spiritual aroma or aura of which is religion. In the perspective of the dialectical religiology, if Hegel had still been alive in 1844/1845, he would probably have accepted Marx's radical humanism-naturalism, that man is indeed the root of family, society, state, history, and culture, i. e. art, religion, philosophy, but he would also have asked further for the foundation of man, and if Marx would have answered nature, Hegel would have asked·for the root of nature, the logic, because for him family, society, state, history, and culture concretely superseded man, as he determinately sublated nature, and nature superseded God's logic (Genesis 1, 2; John 1; Hegel 1896; 1964; 1965; 1969; 1972; 1976; 1979; 1986a; 1986b; 1986c; 1986e; 1986f; 1986g; 1986h; 1986i; 1986j; 1986l; 1986m; 1986n; 1986o; 1986p; 1986q; 1986r; 1986s; 1986t; Feuerbach 1904; 1957; 1996; Marx 1953: 207; Marx/Engels 1955; 1960; 2005; Horkheimer 1972:chap 4; Habermas 1969; 1970; 1973; 1976; 1977; 1978a;

1978e; 1978d; 1984a; 1986; 1978b; 1988a; 1990; 1992a; Küng 1970; 1978; Siebert 1970; 1972a; 1972b; 1973a; 1973b; 1973c; 1975b; 1977; 1980; 1981; 2010b; Moore 2009; Ferguson 2010). For Hegel, God's logic and the worlds logic were still the same. The critical theory of religion still asks these questions, which Hegel may have asked his disciple Marx, and is precisely therefore more *radical* even than Marx (Siebert 1965; 1966; 1970; 1972a; 1972b; 1973a; 1973b; 1973c; 1975b; 1977; 1978; 1979a; 1979c; 1979d; 1980; 1981; 1985; 1987a; 1987b; 1987d; 1989; 1994a; 1994c; 1994d; 1995; 2000; 2001; 2002a; 2010b; Moore 2009; Ferguson 2010).

Protestation against Misery

For Marx, the religious misery, which he saw around himself in the bourgeois world, was at the same time the expression of the real proletarian misery in antagonistic civil society, and the protestation against this real misery (Hegel 1986g: 339-397; 1986l: 491-560; 1986p; 1986q; Marx 1953:208-209; Lefebvre 1982; Moore 2009; Ferguson 2010; Baron 2011: 65-68;Kesting 2011:68-70;Hochgeschwender 2010;Keegan 2010; MacPherson 2010).. Religion was dialectical in itself. The religion was ideology, understood critically as false consciousness and the masking of particularistic national and class interests, as well as its opposite, the sigh of the oppressed creature. Religion was the heart of a heartless capitalistic world. Religion was the spirit of spiritless bourgeois conditions. Religion was the opiate not for but rather of the people. Marx's 6 definitions of religion show, that he was unlike supposedly Weber or Habermas not at all *religiously un-musical* (Hegel 1986g: 339-397; 1986l: 491-560; 1986p; 1986q; Marx 1953:208-209; Weber 1952; 1962; 1963; 1969; 1978; 1992; 2002; Arens 1995; 1997; 2007; 2009; Arens/John/Rottländer 1991; Zizek 2007; 2009; Zizek/ Milbank 2008; Moore 2009; Ferguson 2010). Even Marx's last opiate-definition, which usually alone is quoted by bourgeois scholars, shows a sensitivity for religion: what is wrong with taking an opiate against extreme pain and suffering in any slum of any American city, was that it may disable the proletariat to change its miserable conditions and abolish itself? In the perspective of the dialectical theory of society and religion, informed by Marx, religion is dialectical in itself: there is not only a dialectic between the sacred and the profane, but also a dialectic in the enlightenment and a dialectic in the religion, which are awaiting their resolution and reconciliation (Moore 2009; Ferguson 2010; Siebert 2010).

Happiness

According to Marx, the naturalistic-humanistic annulment, repeal, abolishment, or cancellation of ideological religion as the illusionary happiness of the people was the demand for their genuine, real happiness (Hegel 1986g: 339-397; 1986l: 491-560; 1986p; 1986q; Marx 1953:208-209; Lefebvre 1982; Weber 1952; 1962; 1963; 1969; 1978; 1992; 2002; Arens 1995; 1997; 2007; 2009; Arens/John/Rottländer 1991; Zizek 2007; 2009; Zizek/Milbank 2008; Thierse 2011: 20-23; Moore 2009; Ferguson 2010; Siebert 2010b). For Marx, the humanistic-naturalistic demand, that the people should give up the religious illusions about their miserable condition, is the demand to give up a condition, which is in need of illusions (Hegel 1986p; 1986q; Marx 1953:208-209; Fromm 1950; 1966b; 1967; 1980b; 1981; 1990b; 1992; 1997; 1999; 2001; Moore 2009; Ferguson 2010). A sane, good, and truly happy society would be one, which would no longer need the continual canonization of heroes or saints, be it in Rome or elsewhere (Hegel 1986p; 1986q; Marx 1953:208-209; Fromm 1950; 1966b; 1967; 1980b; 1981; 1990b; 1992; 1997; 1999; 2001; Rudolphi 1949; Weitensteiner 2002; Moore 2009; Ferguson 2010; Siebert 1993). The proletarian saint would be the last in the history of sainthood (Hegel 1896p;

1986q; Rudolphi 1949; Weitensteiner 2002; Moore 2009; Ferguson 2010; Siebert 1993). Thus, in Marx's perspective, the naturalistic-humanistic critique of religion was in its very core the critique of the miserable capitalist *valley of tears*, the halo of which was religion (Marx 1953:208-209). In view of the critical religiology, Marx's critique was directed against religion insofar as it had turned into ideology, understood critically as untruth (Marx 1953: chaps, V, VI, VIIIX; Adorno 1970b; Moore 2009; Ferguson 2010).

The Rose in the Cross

Hegel had stated in his idealistic philosophy of law, that what stood between the reason as self-conscious spirit, and the Reason as present reality, what differentiated the former reason from the latter, and what did not allow people to find satisfaction in the latter, was the fetter of some kind of an abstraction, which had not been liberated yet into the dialectical notion (Hegel 1964; 1986c; 1986f; 1986h; 1986g: 24 27, 42-43; 1986l:11-141; 1986q:342-344, 347-536; Moore 2009; Ferguson 2010). To recognize the *Reason* as the *Rose in the cross* of the present and thereby to enjoy it, this rational insight was the reconciliation with the present, which the philosophy granted to those people, to whom once had come the internal demand to comprehend, and to receive in that, what was substantial, likewise their subjective freedom, and to stand with the subjective freedom not in some particular and accidental element, but in that, what was in and for itself (Hegel 1986g: 24 27, 42-43; 1986l: 11-141; 1986q: 290-292; Ferguson 2010). For Hegel, what is rational, that is or will be real, and what is real, that is or will be rational (Hegel 1986g: 24-25; Moore 2009; Ferguson 2010). To the contrary, in Marx's view, the historical - materialistic, humanistic - naturalistic critique of religion . had picked to pieces the imaginary flowers, or the rose, on the chain, or on the cross, not so that the man would carry the chain, or the cross, without imagination and consolation, but that he would throw off the chain, or the cross, and break the living flower, or the rose (Hegel 1986g: 24 27, 42-43; 1986q: 290-292; Marx 1871; 1906; 1951; 1953:208; 1956; 1961a; 1961b; 1961c; 1963; 1964; 1974; 1977; 2000; ; Marx/Engels 1953a; 1953b; 1953c; 1955; 1960; 2005; Lefebvre 1982; Moore 2009; Ferguson 2010). The humanistic-naturalistic critique of religion disappointed the man, so that he may think, and act, and form and shape his reality like a disappointed man, who had come to his senses and understanding: so that he may move around himself, and thereby around his real sun. In Marx's view, the religion was only the illusionary sun, which turned around man, as long as he did not move around himself (Marx 1871; 1906; 1951; 1953:208; 1956; 1961a; 1961b; 1961c; 1963; 1964; 1974; 1977; 2000; ; Marx/Engels 1953a; 1953b; 1953c; 1955; 1960; 2005; Lefebvre 1982; Moore 2009; Ferguson 2010).

Naturalistic-Humanistic Position

In the perspective of the dialectical religiology, Marx moved - in a *quasi-Copernican* sense - from the Hegelian, Biblical, theistic position to a post-theistic socialistic- humanistic-naturalistic position (Hegel 1986g: 24 27, 42-43; 1986q: 290-292; Marx 1953: 208; Bloch 1960; 1970a; 1970b; 1971a; 1971b; 1972; 1975a; 1975b 1975c; 1985c; 1985b; 1985c; 1985d; 1985e; 2009; Bloch/Reif 1878; Fromm 1932a; 1932b; 1950; 1956; 1957; 1959; 1964; 1966a; 1966b; 1966c; 1967; 1968; 1970a; 1970b; 1972a; 1972b; 1973; 1974; 1975; 1976; 1980a; 1980b; 1981; 1990a; 1990b; 1992; 1995; 1997; 1999: 34-36; Fromm/ Suzuki/Martino 1960; Feomm/Xirau; Benjamin 1977:chaps 10, 11; Horkheimer 1972 chaps. 1-6, 7; 1985l: 294-296, 483-492; Brecht 1961; 1964; 1966; 1967; 1980; 1981; 1994; 2002; 2003; 2007a; 2007b; Habermas 1969; 1970; 1976; 1977; 1978a; 1978c; 1978d; 1982; 1984a; 1986; 1987a; 1987b; 1987c; 1988a; 1988b; 1990; 1991a: part III; 1991c; 1992b; 1992c; 1997a;

1997b; 1999; 2001a; 2001c; 2002; 2003b; 2004b; 2005; 2006a; 2006b; 2007; Habermas/Bovenschen 1981; Habermas/ Henricch 1974; Habermas/Ratzinger 2006; Thierse 2011: 20-23; Nida-Rümen 2011: 23-25; Moore 2009; Ferguson 2010). Man becomes the center for man, but not necessarily in an idolatrist, but rather in a relative sense: there is something after communism (Isaiah 65; Fromm 1950; 1956; 1959; 1966b; 1967; 1970b; 1974; 1976; 1980b; 1992; 1995; 1997; 1999; 2001; Lundgren 1998; Moore 2009; Ferguson 2010). There will be no miserable *tenement houses* or *projects* any longer for the proletariat in New York, or in any other city (Moore 2009; Ferguson 2010; Siebert 2010b). There will be no proletariat or precariate any longer. Persons, groups, nations, and states will recognize each other, and treat each other in mutual respect, and according to the Golden Rule, or the categorical imperative, or the *apriori* of the unlimited communication community, be it in Palestine, Israel, the Near East, Africa, or elsewhere (Matthew 5-7; Luke 6; Apel 1975; 1976a; 1976b; 1982; 1990; Habermas 1962; 1969; 1970; 1971; 1973; 1975; 1976; 1977; 1978a; 1978c; 1978d; 1983; 1984a; 1985a; 1986; 1987c; 1988b; 1991a; 1991b; 1992a; 1992c; 2001a; 2002; Spencer 2011; Moore 2009; Ferguson 2010). However, neither humanism nor naturalism must turn into idolatry (Horkheimer/Adorno 1951: 284-211; 1956; 1969a; 1969b; 1972a; 1972b; 1984; 2002; Lundgren 1998 Moore 2009; Ferguson 2010). Neither nature, man, or history will be absolutized and considered to be ultimate. There will continue the longing, that the world of appearance with all its injustices may not be the last word (Horkheimer 1985g: chap. 37; Moore 2009; Ferguson 2010). . Beyond finite nature and its evolution, and beyond finite man and his history, there will still be the totally Other than both, and their finite logic, and their laws, and their horror and their terror, their tsunamis, hurricanes and tornados, and their wars, where once in the *System* there was situated the logic as logos -theology and – theodicy, and no longer will the notions abstracted from nature in the history of mythology and philosophy and science be projected into it as the thoughts of God before creation, but these projections will be taken back into the human mind, where they came from, and nature's and man's logic will be different from God's Logic, and there will be more difference than similarity in the *analogia entis* (Hegel. 1891; 1964; 1979; 1986c; 1986e; 1986f; 1986h; 1986i; 1986j; 1986p; 1986q; 1986r; 1986s; 1986t; Moore 2009; Ferguson 2010; Siebert 2010b). Often theology contained already in itself a humanistic-naturalistic moment: the consideration for the poor classes (Isaiah 2, 3, 11, 14. 19, 24, 25, 27, 28, 30-33, 35, 55, 60, 65, 66; Marx 1953 208-209; Moore 2009; Ferguson 2010). As this humanistic-naturalistic element becomes thematic and central in terms of the abolishment of the poor classes and their misery, it must ally itself precisely now with theology, in order to avoid idolatry, and to be able to resolve its metaphysical problems (Benjamin 1977: chaps 10 and 11; Adorno 1970b; Lundgren 1998; Zizek 2007; 2009; Zizek/Milbank 2008; Moore 2009; Ferguson 2010; Siebert 2919b).

The Task

According to Marx, it was the task of history, to establish after the Beyond of truth had disappeared, the truth of this-worldliness (Marx 1953: 208-209; Moore 2009; Ferguson 2010). It was first of all the task of philosophy, which stands in the service of history, after the sacred form of human self-estrangement had been unmasked, to expose the secular self-alienation in its unholy forms Thereby, the critique of heaven, or the religious, transforms itself into the critique of the earth, or the secular, the critique of religion into the critique of profane law,, and the critique of theology into the critique of secular politics . In the perspective of the dialectical religiology, it may also happen that the concretely superseded theology may be in the service of historical materialism and *vice versa* and that its task may be to help to realize not alternative Future I - the alienated totally administered society, or alternative Future II - the estranged, completely militarized society, but rather alternative Future III - the realm of freedom on the basis of the realm of natural and economic necessity, a just society as long anticipated by the Hebrew prophets, and in Plato's *Politeia*, in Aristotle's *Nikomachian Ethics*, in Hobbes's *Leviathan*, in Lockes' *Second Treatise*, in Rousseau's *Contract Social* and in Kant's *On Eternal Peace* and long after Marx, only 40 years ago, in John Rawls's *Theory of Justice*, which society would also not be ultimate and infinite, but rather finite and transitory (Marx 1961: 873-874; Flechtheim 1959: 625-634; 1862: 27-34; 1963: 148-150; 1966: 455-464; 1971; Flechtheim/ Lohmann 2003; Horkheimer 1985g: chaps. 34; 35; 36; 37; 4o; Thierse 2011: 20-23; Nida-Rümelin 2011: 23-25; Neian 2011: 48-51; Maas 2011: 51-54; Meier 2011: 61-64'Moore 2009; Ferguson 2010; Baron 2011: 65-68;Kesting 2011:68-70;Hochgeschwender 2010;Keegan 2010; MacPherson 2010).

Critical Theology

According to Marx's *Economic and Philosophic Manuscripts of 1844*, it was only with Feuerbach that the positive, humanistic and naturalistic criticism of the religious and the secular began (Feuerbach 1904; 1957; 1996; Marx 1951; 1953: chap VI; Moore 2009; Ferguson 2010). In Marx's view, the less noise Feuerbach's writings made, the more certain, profound, extensive and enduring was their effect. Marx saw in them the only writings since Hegel's *Phenomenology* and *Logic* to contain a real theoretical revolution (Hegel 1896; 1964; 1986c; 1986e; 1986f; 1986h; 1986j; Feuerbach 1904; 1957; 1996; Moore 2009; Ferguson 2010). In contrast to the critical theologians of 1844, Marx deemed the concluding chapter of his own *Economic and Philosophic Manuscripts of 1844*, entitled *Critique of the Hegelian Dialectic and Philosophy as a Whole* to be absolutely necessary (Hegel 1896; 1964; 1986c; 1986e; 1986f; 1986h; 1986j; Feuerbach 1904; 1957; 1996 Marx 1951:2; 1953: chap VI; Moore 2009; Ferguson 2010). This task had not yet been performed by 1844. For Marx, this lack of thoroughness was not accidental, since even the critical theologian remained a theologian. Hence, so Marx argued, either the critical theologian has to start from certain presuppositions of philosophy, accepted as authoritatively, or the critical theologian, if in the process of criticism and as a result of other peoples 's discoveries doubts about these philosophical presuppositions have arisen in him, he abandoned them in a cowardly and unwarrantable fashions. The critical theologian abstracted from the philosophical presuppositions, thus showing his servile dependence on them, and his resentment at this servility merely in a negative, unconscious, and sophistical manner. In the perspective of he critical religiology, while with Hegel Jerusalem and Athens, theology and philosophy, Biblical religion and ontology were still united, Feuerbach and Marx tore them apart and de-Hellenized them, as the Reformation, and the bourgeois enlightenment had done before the Marxist enlightenment and revolutions, and as the multi-culturalism does today in 2011 (Hegel 1896; 1964; 1986c; 1986e; 1986f; 1986h; 1986j; Feuerbach 1904; 1957; 1996; Marx 1951:2; 1953: chap VI; Horkheimer/Fromm/ Marcuse 1936; Fromm 1967; Marcuse 1960; 1961; 1962; 1970; Habermas 1969; 1970; 1971; 1973; 1976; 2001a; 2002; 2004b; 2006a; 2006b; 2007; Habermas/Henrich 1974; Habermas/ Ratzinger 2006; . Tillich 1926; 1929; 1933; 1948; 1951; 1952-1955a; 1955b; Lortz 1962a; 1962b; 1964; Thierse 2011: 20-23; Nida-Rümelin 2011: 23-25; Neian 2011: 48-51; Maas 2011: 51-54; Moore 2009; Ferguson 2010; Siebert 1965; 2005; 2010b)

.

Idealism as Idolatry

In Marx's perspective, the critical theologian did his work either by constantly repeating assurances concerning the purity of his own criticism, or by trying to make it seem as though all that was left for criticism to deal with now, was some other limited form of criticism outside itself. Marx thought of the 18th century bourgeois criticism (Hegel 1896; 1964; 1986c; 1986e; 1986f; 1986h; 1986j; Feuerbach 1904; 1957; 1996 Marx 1951:2; 1953: chap VI; 2000; Marx/ Engels 2005; Fromm1966b; 1967; Adorno/Kogon 1958a: 392-402; 1958b: 484-498; Moore 2009; Ferguson 2010). The critical theologian also pointed - like Hegel before- to the limitations of the masses in civil society, in order to divert the observer's attention as well as his own from the necessary task of settling accounts between criticism and its point of origin: namely the Hegelian dialectical logic as logos theology, and German idealistic philosophy as a whole - i. e. from the *idolatry* of human self-consciousness and the projection of the human mind into the Absolute, the absolute Spirit (Exodus 20; Hegel 1896; 1964; 1986c; 1986e; 1986f; 1986h; 1986j; Feuerbach 1904; 1957; 1996 Marx 1951:2; 1953: chap VI; 2000; Bloch 1960; 1970a; 1970b; 1971a; Fromm 1950; 1959; 1966a; 1966b; 1967; Flechtheim/Lohmann 2003; Lungren 1993; Moore 2009; Ferguson 2010). In the perspective of the dialectical theory of society and religion, such charge of idolatry can be made only from the theistic position of the Abrahamic religions, or of their concrete post-theistic supersession (Exodus 20; Hegel 1896; 1964; 1986c; 1986e; 1986f; 1986h; 1986j; Feuerbach 1904; 1957; 1996; Marx 1951:2; 1953: chap VI; Fromm1950; 1959; 1966a; 1966b; 1967; Flechtheim /Lohmann 2003; Lungren 1993; Küng 1978; 1991b; 1994a; 1994b; 2004; Moore 2009; Ferguson 2010). Who ever speaks about idolatry, must include its opposite: a genuine theology as *idology*, which arrives through the negation of the negative, the idols, at the affirmation of the imageless and nameless Eternal One, or totally Other than nature and man and the whole finite world of appearances (Exodus 20; Horkheimer 1971; 1985g: chaps. 17; 29; 37, 40; Horkheimer/Adorno 1969a; 1969b; 1972a; 1972b; 1984; 2002; Fromm 1950; 1959; 1966a; 1966b; 1967; Flechtheim /Lohmann 2003; Lungren 1993; Moore 2009; Ferguson 2010; Ferguson 2010; Siebert 2019b). According to Marx, the critical theologian diverted attention from this necessary task, to raise modern criticism above its own limitation and crudity: its idealistic *idolatry* (Exodus 20; Horkheimer 1936; 1971; 1985g: chaps 17; 29; 37, 40; Horkheimer/Adorno 1969a; 1969b; 1972a; 1972b; 1984; 2002; Fromm1950; 1959; 1966a; 1966b; 1967; Flechtheim /Lohmann 2003; Lungren 1993; Moore 2009; Ferguson 2010; Siebert 2019b). Such critical idology was indeed Marx's and Freud's greatest contribution to a truly critical theology as theodicy: a genuine Jewish contribution in spite of all the conformist neo-liberal Friedmann's and *Greenspans* (Exodus 20; Bloch 1960; 1970a; 1970b; 1971a; Horkheimer 1936; 1971; 1985g: chaps 17; 29; 37, 40; Horkheimer/Adorno 1969a; 1969b; 1972a; 1972b; 1984; 2002; Fromm1950; 1959; 1966a; 1966b; 1967; Flechtheim /Lohmann 2003; Lungren 1993; Oelmüller 1990; 1992; Moore 2009; Ferguson 2010; Siebert 2019b); This continual struggle against idolatry as the source of all other sins – stealing, murdering, lying, etc. - rather than the nomadic life style of the Hebrews, seems to be the general theme in all variations of Anti-Semitism, or better still Anti-Judaism in Antiquity, Middle Ages, and Modernity (Horkheimer 1936; 1971; 1985g: chaps. 17; 29; 37, 40; 1985l: 172-183; Horkheimer/Adorno 1969a; 1969b; 1972a; 1972b; 1984; 2002; Fromm1950; 1959; 1966a; 1966b; 1967; Flechtheim/Lohmann 2003; Lungren 1993; Moore 2009; Moore 2009; Ferguson 2010; Siebert 2019b);

Discoveries

According to Marx, eventually, however, whenever discoveries, like those e. g. of Feuerbach's projection theory, were made regarding the nature of the critical theologian's own philosophic presuppositions, he partly made it appear, as if he were the one, who had accomplished them, producing that appearance by taking the results of these discoveries and, without being able to develop them, hurling them in the form of slogans or catch-phrases at writers still caught up in the confines of subjective, -objective, -absolute-idealistic philosophy (Kant 1929; 1946; 1968; 1970; 1974a; 1974b; 1975; 1981; 1982; 1983; Hegel 1986h; 1986i; 1986j; Feuerbach 1904; 1957; 1996; Marx 1951; 1953: chap. VI; 1964; 1974; 2009; Levebvre 1982; Moore 2009; Ferguson 2010). The critical theologian partly even managed to acquire a sense of his own superiority to such discoveries by asserting in a mysterious way, and in a veiled malicious and skeptical fashion elements of the Hegelian dialectical logic, which he still found lacking in the criticism of that dialectic, and which have not yet been critically served up to him for his use, against such criticism - not having tried to bring such elements into their proper relation, or having been able of doing so, asserting, lets say, the category of *mediating proof* against the category of *positive self-originating truth*, in a way peculiar to Hegelian dialectic (Hegel 1964; 1972; 1979; 1986a; 1986b; 1986c; 1986e; 1986f; 1986h; 1986j; 1986t; Marx 2000; Moore 2009; Ferguson 2010). . For to the theological critic it seemed quite natural, that everything had been done by idealistic philosophy, so that he could chatter away about purity, resoluteness, and quite critical criticism Thus, the critical theologian fancied himself the true conqueror of idealistic philosophy, whenever he happened to feel some dialectical element of Hegel lacking in Feuerbach. For, however much the critical theologian practiced the spiritual idolatry of self-consciousness and mind, he did not get beyond feeling to consciousness in terms of Hegel's *Phenomenology of Mind* (Hegel 1986c; Feuerbach 1904; 1957; 1996; Marx. 2000; Moore 2009; Ferguson 2010).

Religious Transcendence

Marx had to admit on closer inspection, that the theological criticism - movement had been genuinely progressive at its inception and beginning (Hegel 1986c; Feuerbach 1904; 1957; 1996; Marx. 2000, Moore 2009; Ferguson 2010). But in the final analysis, Marx saw the critical theology to be nothing else, but the culmination and consequence of the old idealistic-philosophical and especially Hegelian *Transcendentalism,* twisted into a theological caricature. For Marx, this was an interesting example of historical justice, which now assigned to theology, which had always been the idealistic philosophy's *spot of infection,* the further role of portraying in itself the negative dissolution of idealistic philosophy, i. e. the process of its decay: a historical *nemesis.* Marx had to admit in his further exposition, that on the other hand Feuerbach's discoveries about the nature of philosophy did still call - for their proof at least - for a critical discussion of philosophical dialectic. In the view of the dialectical religiology, indeed, the critical theologians, in so far as they have really been critical and progressive, and thus have liberated themselves from the *idolatry of human self-consciousness,* and do no longer project the human mind into the divine Spirit, remain still theologians, because Hegel's untwisted *Transcendentalism,* freed from all idolatrous, anthropomorphic projections, remains precisely that, not as a positive, but rather as a negative eschatological notion: the *Highest Idea, including being; Ens a se ;* the *Divine One as the negation of negations, and the desire of desires, and the denial of denials;* the *One who denies of every other that it is anything* except himself; the *One to which nothing is to be added;* the *Not-God;* the *No-Ghost;* the *Apersonal, Aspiritual,*

Formless One, who is pure, sheer, and limpid and without Duality; the *One, into whom people sink eternally from negation to negation;* the *Thing in itself,* including *God, Freedom and Immortality;* the *Good Infinity;* the *Identity of the Identity and the non-identity; the Supreme Being;* the *Ultimate Reality;* the *Absolute Future;* the *X-Experience;* the imageless and nameless *totally Other,* the *Unconditional,* shortly the *Transcendence* (Isaiah 65, 66; Revelation 21, 22; Anselm 1962; Thomas Aquinas 1922; Blakney 1941: 247-248; Buber 1937; 1952; 1957; 1960; 1965; 1966; 1987a; 1967b; 1968; 1970a; 1970b; 1970c; 1972; 1973a; 1973b; 1983; 1985; 1991a; 1991b; 1992; 1994; 1999b; 1999c; 2002a; 2002b; 2002c; 2002d; 2002e; 2003; Scholem 1935; 1967; 1970a; 1970b; 1973b; 1977a; 1977b; 1977c; 1980; 1982; 1989; Buber 1937; 1952; 1957; 1960; .1965; 1966; 1967a; 1967b; 1968; 1970a; 1970b; 1970c; 1972; 1973a; 1973b; 1983; 1985; 1001a; 1991b; 1992; 1994; 1999b; 1999c; 2002a; 2002b; 2002c; 2002d; 2002e; 2003; Kant 1929; 1946; 1968; 1970; 1974a; 1974b; 1975; 1981; 1982; 1983; Hegel 1986c; 1986h; 1986i; 1986j 1986p; 1986q; Marx 1953:. 227-228; 269-316; Benjamin chaps. 10, 11; Horkheimer 1936; 1967b; 1985g: chaps. 17; 29; 37; 1985l: 483-493; Habermas 1969/1970; 1976; 1977; 1978a; 1988a; 1988b; 1991a; 1992b; 1992c; 2002; Metz 1959; 1962; 1967; 1970; 1972a; 1972b; 1973a; 1973b; 1973c; 1975b; 1977; 1980; 1995; 1997; 1998; Metz/Habermas/Sölle 1994; Metz/Wiesel 1993; Küng 1978; Küng/Homolka 2009; Baum 1959; 1967; 1968; 1971; 1972; 1975a; 1975b; 1980a; 1980b; 1982; 1991; 1994; 1996; 2001; 2002; 2003; 2004; 2005; 2007; 2009; Baum (ed) 1999; Gutierrez 1973; 1988; Haag 1981; 1982; 1983; 2005; Siebert 1010b). This negative-theological *Transcendence* remains after Marx had, with the help of Feuerbach, taken the theological content – *Being, Essence, Notion* - out of Hegel's Logos-theology, and had put it back, where it had supposely come form, into the human mind (Hegel 1986c; Feuerbach 1904; 1957; 1996; Marx. 2000). Lenin transformed Hegel's still theological logic into the secular *Alphabet of Revolution* (Lenin 1972:85-244; 317-321; Horkheimer 1987b:295-308-318-319; 1987k: 100-118 171-188). It is not accidental, that even up to the present - 2011- Hegel's idealistic logic has still not yet been replaced by a historical - materialistic one (Hegel 1986c; 1986e; 1986f; Horkheimer/Adorno 2002). What, according to Habermas, has connected the religious and the secular, ethical monotheism and radical enlightenment, throughout modernity, has been that moment of human Self-Crossing - Over, Self-Exceeding, or Transcendence, which opens up, admits and concedes first of all for the *Ego*, which is caught up in its environments, the distance to the world in its totality, and to itself, without which can not be acquired personal autonomy or universal, i. e. anamnestic, present, and proleptic solidarity on the basis of a linguistically mediated mutual recognition of and respect for each other's dignity. (Freud 1939; 1946; 1955; 1962a; 1962b; 1964; 1969; 1977; 1992; 1993; 1995a; 1995b; Fromm 1859; 1967; 1970b; 1974; 1980b; Adorno/Kogon 1958a:392-402; 1958b:484-498; Habermas 1990: 14-15; Küng 1978; 1990a ; Moore 2009; Ferguson 2010). The acceptance of such Transcendence shared by believers and enlighteners, does in no way touch upon the conviction of the critical theorists of society, that nothing of theological content will continue unchanged in history (Adorno/Kogon 1958a:392-402; 1958b:484-498; Habermas 1990: 14-15; Moore 2009; Ferguson 2010). Every theological content has to expose itself to the test, to migrate into the secular dimension. But this secularizing bringing of theological contents into the universe of argumentative discourse, and solidary living together, and cooperation, is the very opposite of the neo-pagan regression behind the self-understanding of personal autonomy and universal solidarity, which entered world history through the Jewish, Christian, and Islamic prophetic teachings (Isaiah 56-66; Matthew 5-7; Revelation 21-22; The Holy Qur'an Sura I-IV;

Adorno/Kogon 1958a: 392-402; 1958b:484-498; Habermas 1990: 14-15; Küng 1991b; 1994a. ; 1994b; 2004; Byrd 2011 Moore 2009; Ferguson 2010). Hegel's, Hölderlin's, and Schelling's *Mythology of Reason* had concretely superseded into itself the prophetic teachings of the Abrahamic religions. (Hegel 1972; 1979; 1986a; 1986b; . Habermas 1990: 14-15; Moore 2009; Ferguson 2010). This mythology of reason has nothing to do with the contemporary fascist or neo-conservative praise of a this-worldly polytheism or pagan mythologies, which terminate the majority of the human subject, and which have been spread through out late capitalist society in fascist and liberal form. Marx was as little willing or able, to dissolve the religious into the secular without residual, as the old Rabbis - or for that matter- the orthodox Priests, Bishops, or Ministers, Imams, or Ayatollahs - were able to dissolve the profane into the sacred through sanctification (Leviticus 19:2; 20:7-9, 10-12; Lieber 2001: 693, 701-702; Hegel 1965; 1969; 1972; 1986j; 1096p: 9-88; 1986q; 1986r; 1986s; 1986t; Otto 1969; 1991; Eliade 1961; Adorno 1963; 1969a; 1969b; 1993c; Küng 1978; 1991b; 1994a; 1994b; 2004; Byrd 2011; Cessna 2011: 1-6 Moore 2009; Ferguson 2010). If religion has ever made substantial contributions to the humanization of man, and if the secularization of individual, family, society, state, history, and culture can - in spite of some sporadic counter-revolutionary appearances of de-secularization and return to religion e. g. in Eastern Europe - can not be stopped in the long run, then - in order to help to resist utter barbarism - progressive semantic material and potentials are to be rescued from the depth of religion and the mythos by an inverse cipher theology into the secular discourse of the expert cultures, and through it into communicative practice in the life world and even into the instrumental action in the economic and political subsystems of the modern systems of human condition, and action systems, otherwise characterized by functional rationality, and run over the media of money and power, and into social movements, which are directed against the inner colonization of the life world by the economic and political subsystems (Parsons 1964: chaps. 1, 2; 1965: chaps 1, 2; 1971; Parsons/Shils 1951; Adorno 1970b; Karpov 2011; Habermas 1962; 1969; 1970; 1971; 1973; 1975; 1976; 1977; 1978a; 1978c; 1978d; 1982; 1983; 1984a; 1984b; 1985a; 1985b; 1986; 1987a; 1987b; 1987c; 1987d; 1988al 1988b; 1990; chap 1; 1991a; 1991b; 1991c; 1992a; 1992b; 1992c; 1997a; 1997b; 1998; 1999; 2001a; 2001b; 2001c; 2002; 2003a; 2003c; 2004a; 2004b; 2004c; 2005; 2006a; 2006b; 2006d; 2007; 2009; Moore 2009; Ferguson 2010; Siebert 1966; 1978; 1979a; 1979b; 1979c; 1979d; 1979e; 1980; 1985; 1986; 1987a; 1987b; 1987c; 1987d; 1989; 1993; 1994a; 1994c; 1994d; 1995; 2001; 2002a; 2002b; 2004a; 2004b; 2005b; 2010b) . While there is no possibility of an idealistic return of the secular to the religious, there is, nevertheless, the possibility, that progressive religious elements may be rescued in secular form (Hegel 1986q; Habermas 1976; 1978c; 1982; 1988b; 1990: chap1; 1991a; part III; 1992c; 2001a; 2002; 2004b; 2005; 2006a; 2006b; 2007; Habermas/Ratzinger 2006; Haag 1981; 1982; 1983; 2005; Moore 2009; Ferguson 2010; Siebert 2010b).

IV. Socialist Decision

During the 20th century, the Protestant theologian and philosopher of history, Paul Tillich, who was not only influenced by Schelling and Hegel, but also by Marx, and without whom Max Horkheimer could not have taken over the directorship of the Institute for Social Research in Frankfurt a. M:, and the critical theory of society could not have been developed, at least not in the way it has been, and who as brave anti-fascist went into exile with the Jewish critical theorists, tried to reconcile through a radical humanistic, existential reinterpretation of both sides of the modern antagonisms between Jerusalem and Athens, between theology and philosophy, between Biblical religion and ontology, and finally between the religious and the secular in late capitalist society (Hegel 1986p; 1986q; Tillich 1926; 1929; 1933; 1948; 1951; 1952; 1955a; 1955b; 1957; 1963a; 1963b; 1966; 1972. 1977; 1983; Stone/Weaver 1998; Moore 2009; Ferguson 2010). According to Horkheimer and Adorno, who had written under Tillich his doctoral thesis on Sören Kierkegaard, the theological work of the great thinker and friend constituted the last trace of theology in the traditional systematic and symbolical sense (Tillich 1926; 1929; 1933; 1948; 1951; 1952; 1955a; 1955b; 1957; 1963a; 1963b; 1966; 1972. 1977; 1983; Stone /Weaver 1998; Horkheimer 1985g: chaps 14; 15; 16; 17; 18; 20; 21; 25; 16; 29; 30; 32; 34; 37; Adorno 1962; Moore 2009; Ferguson 2010). When Paulus visited Western Michigan University, where this essay is written, in 1960, he asked his former student and assistant, the late Dean and Vice-President Cornelius Loew, what would become of his systematic theological work? Cornelius, who had translated and edited much of it, answered: nothing,, because Americans can not think systematically. Paulus' wife Hannah counseled his students, who later on became professors at Western Michigan University, not to study theology, but rather move into art or into *Religionswissenschaft* instead. They chose the comparative religiology instead of theology. The students participated in Seminars at the University of Chicago, which were taught by Tillich and Mircea Eliade. The students did not follow the religious socialist Tillich, because his theology was too systematic, but rather the religious fascist Eliade (Tillich 1933; 1977; 1983; Eliade 1961). The students did not know, that Tillich had written the *Socialist Decision* in Sils Marie, where Nietzsche had composed his Zarathustra in 1933, before he emigrated from fascist Germany to the USA, in spite of the fact that he considered this book to be his greatest work (. (Tillich 1933; 1977; 1983 Moore 2009;

Ferguson 2010). When Tillich came to America, he kept his best book hidden, because American society was very conservative, and he did not want to hurt his likewise conservative friends, who made great sacrifices, in order to bring him to the States. Since he could not introduce himself to the conservative American society with his *Socialist Decision*, he replaced it with a new book *On the Boundary*, which did not deal with the class antagonism, but rather with the contradiction between the religious and the secular. (Tillich 1966). When Tillich visited Kalamazoo in 1960, he was not aware that from a parish in this town had come the famous and infamous originally Canadian fascist and Anti-Semitic Radio-Priest, Charles Coughlin, the friend of Henry Ford and of Dr. Joseph Goebbels, who represented everything what he fought against throughout his life (Baldwin 2001: chap. 19; Moore 2009; Ferguson 2010).

Ultimate Reality

The theologian Tillich searched for the *Ultimate Reality* in the Biblical religion as well as in ontology, and even in modern secularity (Tillich 1955; Parsons 1964: chaps 1, 2; 1965 chaps. 1. 2; Moore 2009; Ferguson 2010). In his theology, Tillich confronted three symbols of the divine self-manifestation - 1. the Creation, 2. the Christ, and 3. the *Eschaton* - with some ontological concepts (Genesis 1, 2; John 1; Revelation 21. 22; Hegel 1964; 1986c; 1986e; 1986f; 1986h; Tillich 1926; 1929; 1933; 1948; 1951; 1952; 1955a; 1955b; 1957; 1963a; 1963b; 1966; 1972. 1977; 1983; Stone/Weaver 1998; Moore 2009; Ferguson 2010). Tillich found seemingly insuperable contradictions between the theological symbols and the ontological concepts. However, Tillich tried, nevertheless, to show, that such contradictions between theology and ontology were not necessary, and that each of these theological symbols demanded and had received ontological interpretations. In the perspective of the dialectical religiology, informed by Horkheimer and the critical theorists of society, ontology - i. e. talk about Being, Essence and Notion - was rather problematic (Hegel 1964; 1986c; 1986e; 1986f; 1986h; Tillich 1926; 1929; 1933; 1948; 1951; 1952; 1955a; 1955b; 1957; 1963a; 1963b; 1966; 1972. 1977; 1983; Stone/Weaver 1998; Horkheimer 1974: 14). For ontology, Being is the most universal category. But it is questionable, if the Universal is really more essential, and if it is really a greater concern for the people than the Particular or the Singular, as the philosophers of Antiquity, the Middle Ages, and the earlier Modernity have believed (Hegel 1964; 1986e; 1986f; 1986h; Horkheimer 1974: 14). The ontological question is analogous to the social question, if the functions at the peak of the social pyramid, of the system of human condition, or of the human action system, of the ministers of state are really more essential than those of the policeman at the street corner (Parsons 1964; 1965; 1971; Parsons/Shils 1951; Horkheimer 1974: 14; Habermas 1962; 1969; 1973; 1976; 1977; 1978a; 1984a; 1992a; Moore 2009; Ferguson 2010). It is not entirely clear, if the all-embracing policies and decrees of the government and the ministers are really more significant or more wasteful, barren, dull, dreary and desolate, than the settlement or the arbitration of the conflicts between parties in the village inn. It may very well be, that the faith in the Universal is not merely the rationalization of the greatest power, corresponding to the separation of command or order on one hand, and of its execution, or performance, on the other. The concrete supersession of this logical antagonism between the Universal and the Particular had been the main theme of Hegel's philosophy, his logic, his dialectic (Hegel 1964; 1986e; 1986f; 1986h; Horkheimer 1974: 14; Moore 2009; Ferguson 2010). . Hegel succeeded theoretically in the mediation of the Universal and the Particular in the Singular not only in his logic, but also in his philosophy of nature, law, history, art, and religion: especially in his Trinitarian Christology (Hegel 1964; 1986c; 1986e; 1986f; 1986h; 1986p; 1986q; Horkheimer 1974: 14; Küng 1970; Moore 2009; Ferguson 2010). However, in the practical life of late bourgeois society, there remains the question of the rotation of the functions of the constitutional state or of the division of labor in late capitalist or socialist society in general, so that the servant or the maid may for some time become the policeman or police woman, or even the minister of state, and *vice versa*. (Hegel 1964; 1965; 1972; 1976; Marx 2000; Adorno 1932; 1951; 1952; 1963; 1966; 1969a; 1959b; 1970a; 1973b; 1979; 1980a; 1980b; 1991a; 1993b; 1993c; Habermas 1969; 1970; 1973; 1976; 1977; 1978a; 1984a; 1992a; Moore 2009; Ferguson 2010). While Horkheimer had no doubt, that the servant or the maid could accomplish this rotation, but the critical theorist of society doubted seriously if the minister of state could do so (Horkheimer 1974: 14). Tillich followed Hegel's logical mediation of the Universal and the Particular in the Singular theoretically in his theology and in his ontology (Hegel 1964; 1986c; 1986e; 1986f; 1986h; 1986p; 1986q; Tillich 1926; 1929; 1933; 1948; 1951; 1952; 1955a; 1955b; 1957; 1963a; 1963b; 1966; 1972. 1977; 1983; Stone/Weaver 1998; Horkheimer 1974: 14; Moore 2009; Ferguson 2010).

Creation

According to Tillich's theology, first of all, creation by the Word out of nothing described the absolute independence of God as Creator, the absolute dependence of creation, and the infinite gap between them (Genesis 1, 2; Scholem 1935; 1967; 1970a; 1970b; 1973b; 1977a; 1977b; 1977c; 1980; 1982; 1989; Buber 1937; 1952; 1957; 1960; 1965; 1966; 1967a; 1967b; 1968; 1970a; 1970b; 1970c; 1972; 1973a; 1973b; 1983; 1985; 1001a; 1991b; 1992; 1994; 1999b; 1999c; 2002a; 2002b; 2002c; 2002d; 2002e; 2003; Tillich 1926; 1929; 1933; 1948;

1951; 1952; 1955a; 1955b; 1957; 1963a; 1963b; 1966; 1972. 1977; 1983; Stone/Weaver 1998). Tillich had to admit, that the ontological question arose immediately at several points. Tillich had to ask, how the eternal Logos, the principle of God's self-manifestation, was related to the secular contents of the world process (Genesis 1, 2; John 1; Hegel 1896; 1964; 1966; 1969; 1972; 1976; 1979; 1986a; 1986b; 1986c; 1986e; 1986f; 1986g; 1986h; 1986i; 1986j; Haag 1981; 1982; 1983; 2005; Tillich 1926; 1929; 1933; 1948; 1951; 1952; 1955a; 1955b; 1957; 1963a; 1963b; 1966; 1972. 1977; 1983; Stone/Weaver 1998). The classical answer to this question, which was still present in Schelling's and Hegel's philosophy, had been, that the essences, or potentialities, or categories of the secular world, were eternally present in the divine *Spirit* or *Mind* (Genesis 1, 2; John 1; Schelling, . 1860; 1946; 1977a. ; 1977b. 1993. Hegel 1896; 1964; 1966; 1969; 1972; 1976; 1979; 1986a; 1986b; 1986c; 1986e; 1986f; 1986g; 1986h; 1986i; 1986j; Haag 1981; 1982; 1983; 2005; Tillich 1926; 1929; 1933; 1948; 1951; 1952; 1955a; 1955b; 1957; 1963a; 1963b; 1966; 1972. 1977; 1983; Stone/Weaver 1998). This answer had either to be accepted or replaced by another one. Every answer was necessarily again an ontological one.

The Christ

According to Tillich, secondly, the Christological confrontation with ontology had led to the question, if there was a necessary conflict between the universal Logos and the particular Logos, who was present in the personal life of the singular Jesus of Nazareth, as the Christ? (Genesis 1, 2; John 1; Schelling, . 1860; 1946; 1977a; 1977b; 1993; Hegel 1896; 1964; 1966; 1969; 1972; 1976; 1979; 1986a; 1986b; 1986c; 1986e; 1986f; 1986g; 1986h; 1986i; 1986j; 1986q:241-298; Haag 1981; 1982; 1983; 2005; Tillich 1926; 1929; 1933; 1948; 1951; 1952; 1955a; 1955b; 1957; 1963a; 1963b; 1966; 1972. 1977; 1983; Stone/Weaver 1998; Zizek 2007; 2009; Zizek/

Milbank 2008). The *Primordial -Christian, Apocalyptic Paradigm of Christianity,* and the following *Old Church Hellenistic Constellation,* and the *Medieval Roman Catholic Paradigm,* and the *Reformation Protestant Constellation,* did not believe in such an unavoidable conflict between Christology and ontology (. John 1; Hegel 1896; 1964; 1966; 1969; 1972; 1976; 1979; 1986a; 1986b; 1986c; 1986e; 1986f; 1986g; 1986h; 1986i; 1986j; 1986q:241-298; Haag 1981; 1982; 1983; 2005; Tillich 1926; 1929; 1933; 1948; 1951; 1952; 1955a; 1955b; 1957; 1963a; 1963b; 1966; 1972. 1977; 1983; Stone/Weaver 1998; Küng 1970; 1994a; 1994b; Zizek 2007; 2009; Zizek/Milbank 2008). For most Christian paradigms the universal Logos, i. e. the divine self-manifestation, was actively present in everything, that existed in nature and history, because everything was continually made through it; . But only the ultimate divine self-manifestation showed, what Martin Luther had called, the heart of the Divinity, God for man, eternal God-manhood in its very center (Hegel 1986q:241-298; Tillich 1926; 1929; 1933; 1948; 1951; 1952; 1955a; 1955b; 1957; 1963a; 1963b; 1966; 1972. 1977; 1983; Stone/Weaver 1998; Lortz 1962a; 1962b; Küng 1970; 1972; 1976; 1978; 1980; 1991b; 1992; 1993a; 1993b; 1994a; 1994b; 2004). The universal Logos and the particular Logos as the power of a singular personal life were one and the same Logos (Hegel 1986q:241-298; Tillich 1926; 1929; 1933; 1948; 1951; 1952; 1955a; 1955b; 1957; 1963a; 1963b; 1966; 1972. 1977; 1983; Stone/Weaver 1998; Lortz 1962a; 1962b; Küng 1970; 1972; 1976; 1978; 1980; 1991b; 1992; 1993a; 1993b; 1994a; 1994b; 2004). Only against the background of the universal Logos was the particular, singularly, incarnate Logos a meaningful concept (Hegel 1986q:241-298; Tillich 1926; 1929; 1933; 1948; 1951; 1952; 1955a; 1955b; 1957; 1963a; 1963b; 1966; 1972. 1977; 1983; Stone/Weaver 1998). For Tillich, Biblical religion had shown the ontological implications of one of its fundamental assertions in the *Prologue* of the *Fourth Gospel:*

In the beginning was the Word:
The Word was with God
and the Word was God.
He was with God in the beginning.
Through him all things came to be,
not one thing had its beginning but through him.
All that came to be had life in him
and that life was the light of men,
a light that shines in the dark,
a light that darkness could not overpower....

The Word was the true light
that enlightens all men;
and he was coming into the world.
He was in the world
that had its being through him,
and the world did not know him.
He came to his own domain
and his own people did not accept him.
But to all who did accept him
he gave power to become children of God,
to all who believe in he name of him
who was born not out of human stock,
or urge of the flesh,
or will of man,
but of God himself.
The Word was made flesh,
he lived among us,
and we saw his glory,
the glory that is his as the only Son of the Father,
full of grace and truth....

(Genesis 1, 2; John 1, 1-18; Hegel1986q:183-346; Tillich
1926; 1929; 1933; 1948; 1951; 1952; 1955a; 1955b; 1957; 1963a;
1963b; 1966; 1972. 1977; 1983; Stone/Weaver 1998; Küng

1970; 1972; 1976; 1978; 1980; 1991b; 1992; 1993a; 1993b; 1994a; 1994b; 2004; Zizek 2007; 2009; Zizek/Milbank 2008). According to Tillich, ontology was able to receive the Christological question: the place, in which the universal Logos manifested itself particularly, singularly, existentially, and unconditionally. The universal Logos appeared in a particular, singular, concrete form. To say, that Jesus as the Christ was the particular, and singular, concrete place, where the universal Logos became visible, was an assertion of faith, and could be made only by him, who was grasped by the Christ as the manifestation of his ultimate concern (John 1; Hegel 1986q:241-298; Tillich 1926; 1929; 1933; 1948; 1951; 1952; 1955a; 1955b; 1957; 1963a; 1963b; 1966; 1972. 1977; 1983; Stone/Weaver 1998; Küng 1970; 1972; 1976; 1978; 1980; 1991b; 1992; 1993a; 1993b; 1994a; 1994b; 2004; Zizek 2007; 2009; Zizek/Milbank 2008). But it was not an assertion, which contradicted or was strange to the search for Ultimate Reality. For Tillich, the name Jesus the Christ implied an ontology.

Theodicy

John's *Prologue* and its contradictions force upon the dialectical religiologist the dramatic of the theodicy question: the global landscape of screams and shouts (Amos 9: 7-15; Lieber 2001: 7-5-708; John 1; Leibniz 1996; Kant 1929; 1946; 1968; 1970; 1974a; 1974b; 1975; 1981; 1982; 1983; Schopenhauer 1946; 1977; 1989; Hegel 1986l:28 540; 1986p: 88; 1986s: 497; 1986t: 248, 455; Marx 2000; Hitler 1943; 1986; Weber 1952; 1962; 1963: chap.IX;1969; 1978;1992;2002;Rosenbaum 1998; Kogon 1965; 1967; 1995; 2002; 2003a; 2003b; Metz 1972a; 1972b; 1973b; 1980; 1995; Metz/Habermas/Sölle 1994; Metz/ Wiesel 1993; Küng 1991b:726-734; Oelmüller 1990; 1992; Baron 2011: 65-68;Kesting 2011:68-70;Hochgeschwender 2010;Keegan 2010; MacPherson 2010; Siebert 1966; 1993; 2001chap. III; 2002a; Ferguson 2010), If the world was created by God through the universal Logos, where does its darkness come from: all the horror and terror of nature and history, in which almost everybody eats almost everybody (John 1; Schopenhauer 1946; 1977; 1989; Hegel 1986l:28 540; 1986p: 88; 1986q:218-298, 502-536 1986s: 497; 1986t: 248, 455; Marx 2000; Hitler 1943; 1986; Rosenbaum 1998; Kogon 1965; 1967; 1995; 2002; 2003a; 2003b; Metz 1972a; 1972b; 1973b; 1980; 1995; Metz/Habermas/Sölle 1994; Metz/Wiesel 1993; Küng 1991b:726-734; Oelmüller 1990; 1992), . If there exists such secular darkness, can there be a good God and universal Logos at all? But this evil darkness does indeed exist: Auschwitz and Treblinka, Dresden and Hiroshima have really happened. (Hitler 1943; 1986; Rosenbaum 1998; Kogon 1965; 1967; 1995; 2002; 2003a; 2003b; Metz 1972a; 1972b; 1973b; 1980; 1995; Metz/Habermas/Sölle 1994; Metz/Wiesel 1993; Küng 1991b: 726-734; ; Koenigsberg 2011; Oelmüller 1990; 1992; Moore 2009; Ferguson 2010). Thus, can there possibly be a good God and a universal Logos, or is the God of ethical theism dead, indeed? (Hitler 1943; 1986; Rosenbaum 1998; Tillich 1926; 1929; 1933; 1948; 1951; 1952; 1955a; 1955b; 1957; 1963a; 1963b; 1966; 1972; 1977; 1983; Vahanian 1967; 1977; Küng 1991b:726-734; Küng 1970; 1978; 1991a; 1991b; 1992; 1993a; 1993b; 1999a; 1994b; 2004; 2009; Küng/ Homolka 2009; Kuschel/Schlensog 2008; Oelmüller 1990; 1992; Moore 2009; Ferguson 2010). Or is the darkness of the world merely the result of man's sinfulness, or more specifically of the non-acceptance of the Light, of the religious enlightenment, of the particular, singular, incarnate Logos, the Christ, and his teachings, the Sermon the Mount, by a majority of Jews and of humanity (John 1; Tillich 1926; 1929; 1933; 1948; 1951; 1952; 1955a; 1955b; 1957; 1963a; 1963b; 1966; 1972; 1977; 1983; Hitler 1943; 1986; Rosenbaum 1998; Kogon 1965; 1967; 1995; 2002; 2003a; 2003b; Metz 1972a; 1972b; 1973b; 1980; 1995; Metz/Habermas/Sölle 1994; Metz/Wiesel 1993; Küng; 1970; 1978; 1991a; 1991b: 726-734;

1992; 1993a; 1993b; 1999a; 1994b; 2004; 2009; Küng/ Homolka 2009; Küng/Ess/Stietencron/Bechert 1984; Kuschel/Schlensog 2008; Oelmüller 1990; 1992; Moore 2009; Ferguson 2010). But the darkness of the world was there before the Christ, and remained after his historical appearance and disappearance, in spite of the fact, that it could not overpower the Light (John 1; Schopenhauer 1946; 1977; 1989; Hegel 1986l:28 540; 1986p: 88; 1986s: 497; 1986t: 248, 455; Marx 2000; Hitler 1943; 1986; Rosenbaum 1998; Kogon 1965; 1967; 1995; 2002; 2003a; 2003b; Metz 1972a; 1972b; 1973b; 1980; 1995; Metz/Habermas/Sölle 1994; Metz/Wiesel 1993; Küng 1991b:726-734; Moore 2009; Ferguson 2010). Where does the curse of finitude come from? (Hitler 1943; 1986; Rosenbaum 1998; Horkheimer 1974: 4-5, 8, 9-10, 14-15, 17-18, 19-21 28-29, 30, 31, 33, 34, 36, 42, 43, 49, 56, 74, 91-92, 106-107; Koenigsberg 2011; Oelmüller 1990; 1992; Moore 2009; Ferguson 2010 Baron 2011: 65-68;Kesting 2011:68-70;Hochgeschwender 2010;Keegan 2010; MacPherson 2010). Maybe, the infinite God - as the mystics said - could not double himself up and create through the universal Logos another Infinite, and therefore existed the finite and all the perils of human beings: loneliness, abandonment, injustice, meaninglessness, illness, ageing and death (Scholem 1935; 1967; 1970a; 1970b; 1973a; 1973b; 1977a; 1977b; 1977c; 1980; 1982; 1989; Habermas 1969; 1976; 1977; 1978a; 1978c; 1978d; 1982; 1986; 1988a; 1988b; 1990: chap 1; 1991a: part III; 1992b; 1997b; 1999; 2001; 2002; Oelmüller 1990; 1992; Hitler 1943; 1986; Rosenbaum 1998; Ferguson 2010; Moore 2009; Ferguson 2010; Siebert 2010b), Where does the necrophilous and nihilistic capitalism come from, which transforms all particular purposes into means again, and which thingifies, commodifies, instrumentalizes, and functionalizes everything and everybody without an ultimate end (Marx 2000; Hitler 1943; 1986; Rosenbaum 1998; Horkheimer 1967b; 1970a; 1970b; 1971; 1972; 1973; 1974a;

1974b; 1978; 1981a; 1981b; 1981c; 1985g: chaps. 33; 34; 35; 36; 37; 40; Horkheimer (ed) 1970; Adorno 1993b; 1997h; 1997u; Koenigsberg 2011; Oelmüller 1990; 1992; Moore 2009; Ferguson 2010). Without capitalism there would have been no fascism in the 20th century, and its war of revenge and of colonial and empirical thievery, and the cheap - labor - concentration - camps, and the killing of 27 million Russians and 6 million Jews and many others (Marx 2000; Hitler 1943; 1986; Rosenbaum 1998; Adorno; 1997u; Kogon 1965; 1967; 1995; 2002; 2003a; 2003b; Metz 1972a; 1972b; 1973b; 1980; 1995; Metz/Habermas/Sölle 1994; Metz/Wiesel 1993; Küng 1991b:726-734; Koenigsberg 2011; Oelmüller 1990; 1992; Ferguson 2010), At this time - June 20011- there is no adequate theoretical religious or ontological solution to the theodicy problem (Leibniz 1996; Kant 1929; 1946; 1968; 1970; 1974a; 1974b; 1975; 1981; 1982; 1983; Schopenhauer 1946; 1977; 1989; Hegel 1986l:28 540; 1986p: 88; 1986s: 497; 1986t: 248, 455; Marx 2000; Hitler 1943; 1986; Rosenbaum 1998; Kogon 1965; 1967; 1995; 2002; 2003a; 2003b; Metz 1972a; 1972b; 1973b; 1980; 1995; Metz/Habermas/Sölle 1994; Metz/Wiesel 1993; Küng 1991b:726-734; Koenigsberg 2011; Oelmüller 1990; 1992; Moore 2009; Ferguson 2010; Siebert 2011). In the perspective of the dialectical religiology, the transition from the God of theism to the God of post- or non-theism, or naturalistic-humanistic religiosity is caused more by the unresolved theodicy problem than by the theistic God's imprisonment in the antagonism of subjectivity and objectivity (Marx 2000; Hitler 1943; 1986; Rosenbaum 1998; Adorno; 1997u; Kogon 1965; 1967; 1995; 2002; 2003a; 2003b; Tillich 1955: 76-77; Metz 1972a; 1972b; 1973b; 1980; 1995; Metz/Habermas/Sölle 1994; Metz/Wiesel 1993; Küng 1991b:726-734; Koenigsberg 2011; Oelmüller 1990; 1992; Ferguson 2010; Snyder 2011; Soros 2011; Zizek 2007; 2009; Zizej/Milbank 2008; Zizek/Crocket/Davis (eds) 2011; Longerich 2011a; 2011b; Epstein 2011; Angrick/Klein 2011).

God on Trial

The dialectical religiologist remembers, that the Rabbis in Auschwitz did no longer accept the traditional Jewish retaliation theodicy or the test theodicy, but instead put God on trial (Adorno 1997u; Wiesel 1982; 1992;Metz/Wiesel 1993). The Rabbis charged God with having broken the covenant, which promised the Hebrews' protection from their enemies. Yahweh would never forget his covenant (Psalm.111). Quickly he would come to his peoples' rescue, imposing his covenant once and for all. Now the Jewish people called for Adonai in their deepest distress and dispair, and all what came were the SS men, and their dogs, and the gas chambers(Kogon. 1965; 1967; 1995;2002;Metz 1995; Metz/Wiesel 1993). The Rabbinical court suspected even, that God had concluded a new covenant with Adolf Hitler and fascist Germany. After three days the Rabbis found God to be guilty as charged. But after the trial of God the Rabbis and other Jews walked over to the gas chambers holding their hands over their heads.According to the Torah, tte Lord had said to Moses, to take the blasphemer outside the camp, and to let all who were within hearing lay their hands upon his head, and let the whole community atone him(Exodus 20; Leviticus 24: 13-14;Lieber 2001: 732/ 10-1) For the later Rabbis that had been a puzzling incident. It was not clear to them, if the blasphemer had cursed God, or had cursed someone else using the name of God, or had simply pronounced God's name without due reverence..In the view of the critical theory of religion, .no matter if God had blasphemed himself by breaking the Covenants, or if the Rabbis had blasphemed against him by putting him on trial, the last word was atonement-reconciliation. Nevertheles, there were Jews, who after the trial of God never prayed again, and today 89% of the Jewish population of the State of Israel are non-believers and secular, not because of science, but rather because of

Auschwitz (Exodus 20; Leviticus 24: 13-14;Lieber 2001: 732/ 10-1 Adorno 1997u; Wiesel 1982;1992;Metz/Wiesel 1993).The story is of relecvance not only for Jews, but for Christians and Muslims as well, who up to Auschwitz had shared the traditional retaliation - and test - theodicy with the Jews, and who are still concerned with the theodicy problem (Exodus 20; Leviticus 24: 13-14;Lieber 2001: 732/ 10-1; Adorno 1997u; Wiesel 1982;1992; Metz 1980; 1995; Metz/Wiesel 1993 Küng 1991bl; 1994a; 1994b).

Radical Christianity

In the perspective of the dialectical religiology, from its very start, long before Marx and humanist Marxism, critical and radical Christianity protested and rebelled, sometimes almost atheistically, against the darkness of the world, characterized by class-domination and - exploitation, in the name of the religious enlightenment of the universal, and particular, and singular Logos, of Jesus, the Christ (Genesis 1, 2, 3; 4; Psalm 22; Matthew 27: 45-50; Genesis 1, 2, 3; 4; John 1; Hegel 1964; 1965; 1969; 1972; 1976; 1979; 1986a; 1986b; 1986c; 1986e; 1986f; 1986h; 1986j; 1986l; 1986q: 241-298; Marx 1871; 1906; 1951; 1953; 1956; 1961a; 1961b; 1961c; 1963; 1964; 1974; 1977; 2000; Marx/Engels 1953a; 1953b; 1960; 2005; Fromm 1950; 1959; 1964; 1966a; 1966b: chap. ix:; 1967; 1968; 1970b; 1974; 1976; 1980b; 1981; 1990b; 1992; 1995; 1997; 1999; 2001; Lefebvre 1982; Horkheimer1974: 96-97; Fromm (ed) 1966c; Fromm/Suzuki/Martino 1960; Funk 1995; 1999; 2000a; 2000b; Funk/. Joach/ Meyer 2000; Bloch 1960; 1970a; 1970b; 1971a; 1971b; 1972; 1975b 1975c; ; 1985e; 2009; Bloch/Reif 1978; Flechtheim 1971; Flechtheim/Lohmann 2003; Raines/Dean 1970; Buber 1916; 1945; 1950a; 1950b; 1951; 1952a; 1952c; 1953b; 1962; 1965; Sölle 1977; 1992; 1994 Sölle/Habermas etc, . 1975; Sölle/Metz 1990; Metz 1995; Metz/Wiesel 1993; Küng 1991b; 1994a; 1994b; Koenigsberg 2011; Thierse 2011: 20-23; Nida-Rümelin 2011: 23-25; Neian

2011: 48-51; Maas 2011: 51-54; Ferguson 2010; Siebert 2010b). Critical Christianity's revolt even continued at least in the radical religious underground, determined by the Albigenses and Waldenses, by the Franciscans and the Dominicans, by the Brothers of the Free Spirit, by the Edomites, by Thomas Münzer and his revolutionary farmers, etc., even after the authoritarian, hierarchical Christendom went through the Constantinian turn, and allied itself with the Roman state, which had executed Christians on the charges of atheism and high treason for three centuries, and with other states and empires from one Christian paradigm to the other up to the Lateran Treaty with Benito Mussolini, and to the Empire Concordat with Adolf Hitler, which is still valid today - in 2011 - in the German Federal Republic (Engels 1967; Horkheimer 1974:14; Bloch 1960; Raines/Dean 1970: Chap. 1; Lortz 1962: 32, 54, 65, 104, 107-108, 127-128; 184, 244, 349, 514, 531, 551, 793; 799-800, 807, 818, 820, 835; 862, 958; 987, 988, 994-995, 1005; Dirks 1968; 1983a; 1983b; 1985; 1987; 1988; Metz 1970; 1972a; 1972b; 1973b; 1973c; 1975b; 1977; 1978; 1980; 1995; 1997; 1998; ; Metz/Peters 1991; Küng 1991b; 1994a; 1994b; Koenigsberg 2011; Moore 2009; Ferguson 2010; Siebert 1965; 2010b). This radical humanistic Christian underground continued through the anti-fascist priests and ministers of the 20th century, the worker – priests in France, the liberation theologians and the Basic Christian Communities in Central America, etc, while the conservative Christendom allied itself with fascism and neo-liberalism, which as different as they are, nevertheless, share their hate against socialism, and finally produced the present-day neo-conservative Protestant and Catholic radio- and television priests and ministers in Europe and the USA, up to the neo - liberal Fox News, particularly Glenn Beck and Ann Coulter, who think they are redeemed by Jesus, a redemption which they deny to the other party, the Democrats, who supposedly are more secular (Bonhoeffer.

1993; 2000; 2003; Boff 1985; Gutierrez 1973; 1988; Moore 2009; Ferguson 2010). This radical, enlightened, humanistic, revolutionary Christianity continued in the underground, while above the authoritarian, hierarchical, counter-revolutionary Christendom provided ideological legitimation to slaveholders, feudal lords, and capitalists, and consolation to slaves, serfs, and wage laborers (Hegel 1986g; 1986l; 1986p; 1986q; Marx 2000; Bloch 1960, 1970a; 1970b; 1971a; 1971b; 1972; 1975b; 1975c; 1985e; Fromm 1950; 1977; 1959; 1966b; 1967; 1968; 1970b; 1974; 1976; Marcuse 1960; 1961; 1962; 1967; 1965; 1969a; 1969b; 1970a: chap. 1; 1987; 1995; 2001; 2005; Moore 2009; Ferguson 2010).

Eschaton and Eschata

According to Tillich, the third manifestation of God, after creation and Christ, which he confronted with ontological categories, was history, running toward an ultimate end, the historical-eschatological-apocalyptic element in the Abrahamic religions: the *Eschaton* - the community between God and his people in the New Jerusalem - and the *eschata* - no more tears, death, mourning, sadness, and no more breaking of words, worship of obscenities, murderers, fornicators, fortunetellers, idolaters or any other sort of liars. (Isaiah 11, 51, 52, 54, 55, 57, 60, 61, 62, 63, 65, 66, Revelation 21, 22; The Holy Qur'an Sura C - Sura CXIV; Hegel 1964; 1965; 1969; 1972; 1976; 1979; 1986a; 1986b; 1986c; 19863; 1986f; 1986p; 1986q; Tillich 1955: 76-77; Benjamin 1950; 1955a; 1955c; 1968; 1977: chaps 10, 11; Adorno 1970b; Moltmann 1969; 1996; 2002a; 2002b; Metz 1959; 1970; 1972a; 1972b; 1973a; 1973b; 1973c; 1975b; 1977; 1978; 1995; 1997; 1998; ; Metz/Wiesel chaps 10, 11; Küng 1991b; 1994a; 2004; Moore 2009; Ferguson 2010). For Tillich there was the most difficult question, which demanded an ontological answer implied in the historical- eschatological view of the Abrahamic religions. It was the meaning of the Eschaton and the eschata or the relation of the temporal and the Eternal. If people identified the Eternal with the temporal continuation of life after death, they have made a very poor ontological statement by confusing Eternity with endless temporality. (Isaiah 11, 51, 52, 54, 55, 57, 60, 61, 62, 63, 65, 66, Revelation 21, 22; The Holy Qur'an Sura C - Sura CXIV; Hegel 1964; 1965; 1969; 1972; 1976; 1979; 1986a; 1986b; 1986c; 19863; 1986f; 1986p; 1986q; Tillich 1955: 76-77; Benjamin 1950; 1955a; 1955c; 1968; 1977: chaps 10, 11; Adorno 1970b; Moltmann 1969; 1996; 2002a; 2002b; Metz 1959; 1970; 1972a; 1972b; 1973a; 1973b; 1973c; 1975b; 1977; 1978; 1995; 1997; 1998; ; Metz/Wiesel chaps 10, 11; Küng 1978; 1982; 1991b; 1994a; 2004 ; Moore 2009; Ferguson 2010). If people, in opposition to this, say that Eternity is the simple abstract negation of temporality, they have also made a very bad ontological statement by confusing Eternity with timelessness. In Tillich's view, there was, however, a third ontological answer, which does justice to the meaning both of time and of Eternity. According to this third answer, Eternity concretely transcends, i. e. negates and contains temporality, but a temporality which is not subject to the law of finite transitoriness: a temporality, in which past and future are united, though not negated in the eternal Presence. Then history runs toward its ultimate end in the Eternal, and the Eternal participates in the moments of time, judging and elevating them to the Eternal. For Tillich, such statements were ontological in a half-symbolical gown. No theologian could escape them. Those theologians, who still used primitive - mythological language deceived themselves and the people, if they do not realize, that the phrase *life after death* contained an ontology of a highly questionable character. In the perspective of the dialectical religiologist, for Tillich history was not closed, but rather open, as for his friend Benjamin: there was still the possibility of the rescue of the hopeless, and that the murderer would not triumph ultimately over his innocent victim. (Isaiah 11, 51, 52, 54, 55, 57, 60, 61, 62, 63, 65, 66, Revelation 21, 22; The Holy Qur'an Sura C - Sura CXIV; Hegel 1964; 1965; 1969; 1972; 1976; 1979; 1986a; 1986b; 1986c; 19863; 1986f; 1986p; 1986q; Horkheimer 1932; : 125- 144; 1966; 1967a; 1970b; 1971; 2006; ; 1985g: caps 17, 29, 37, 40; Benjamin 1950; 1955a; 1955c; 1968; 1977: chaps 10, 11; Adorno 1970b; Tillich 1955: 76-77; Moltmann 1969; 1996; 2002a; 2002b; Metz 1959; 1970; 1972a; 1972b; 1973a; 1973b; 1973c; 1975b; 1977; 1978; 1995; 1997; 1998; ; Metz/Wiesel chaps 10, 11; Küng 1978; 1982; 1991b; 1994a; 2004; Peukert 1976: 278 293-294, -280; 2009; Ott 2001; 2004a; 2004b; 2004c; 2004d; 2005; 2006; ; Ott (ed) 2007; 2009; Moore 2009; Ferguson 2010; Siebert 2010b).

The God above God

In the perspective of the dialectical religiology, in response to the dramatic, macro-paradigmatic, historical change from Modernity toward Post-Modernity, which started with the end of World War I and has continued through fascism, World War II, neo-liberalism, the Cold War between capitalism and socialism, and the present collision between Islam and secular Western capitalism and socialism, toward alternative Future I - the totally administered society, and alternative Future II - the entirely militarized society, or maybe alternative Future III - the free and reconciled society, and its eclipse of God, Tillich's existential, symbolical theology moved beyond the God of the ethical monotheism of all three Abrahamic religions toward the God of post-theism (Isaiah 11, 51, 52, 54, 55, 57, 60, 61, 62, 63, 65, 66, Revelation 21, 22; The Holy Qur'an Sura C - Sura CXIV; Hegel 1964; 1965; 1969; 1972; 1976; 1979; 1986a; 1986b; 1986c; 19863; 1986f; 1986p; 1986q; Horkheimer 1932: 125-144; 1936; 1966; 1967a; 1970b; 1971; 2006; ; 1985g: caps 17, 29, 34; 35; 36; 37, 40; Benjamin 1950; 1955a; 1955c; 1968; 1977: chaps 10, 11; Adorno 1970b; Fromm 1950; 1959; 1966b; 1967; 1970b;

1974; 1976; 1990b; 1992; 1997; 2001; Flechtheim 1959:625-634; 1962: 27-34; 1963: 148-150; 1966: 4545-464; 1971; Flechteim. Lohmann 2003; Marcuse 1960; 1961; 1962; 1967; 1965; 1969b; 1987; 2001; 2005; Bloch 1960'1970a; 1970b; 1971a; 1971b; 1972; 1975b; 1975c; Habermas 1962; 1969; 1970; 1975; 1976; 1977; 1978a; 1978d; 1981b; 1985b; 1987a; 1988a; 1981c; 1992b; 1992c; 1998; 2001a; 2001b; 2001c; 2003a; 2003b; 2003c; 2004b; 2005; 2006b; 2006c; 2007; 2009; Buber 1952; 1957; 1966; 1967a; 1967b; 1968; 1972; 1973; 1983; 1992; 1994; 1999a; 1999b; 2002a; 2002b; 2002d; 2003; Bin Laden 2005; Byrd 2011; Bonhoeffer 1993; 2000; 2003; Tillich 1955: 76-77; Moltmann 1969; 1996; 2002a; 2002b; Metz 1959; 1970; 1972a; 1972b; 1973a; 1973b; 1973c; 1975b; 1977; 1978; 1995; 1997; 1998; ; Metz/Wiesel chaps 10, 11; Peukert 1976: 278 293-294, -280; 2009; Baum 1967; 1968; 1971; 1972; 1975b; 1980a; 1980b; 1982; 1994; 2004; 2005; 2007; 2009; Baum 1999 (ed); Küng 1978; 1982; 1991b; 1994a; 2004; Peukert 1976: 278 293-294, -280; 2009; Ott 2001; 2004a; 2004b; 2004c; 2004d; 2005; 2006; Ott (ed) 2007; 2009; Thierse 2011: 20-23; Nida-Rümelin 2011: 23-25; Neian 2011: 48-51; Maas 2011: 51-54; Moore 2009; Ferguson 2010; Baron 2011: 65-68;Kesting 2011:68-70;Hochgeschwender 2010;Keegan 2010; MacPherson 2010; Siebert 2010b). According to Tillich, the God above God is the ultimate source of the courage to be in the present world-historical transition period. This was the result of Tillich's demand to determinately negate the traditional theism. Only if the God of theism was concretely transcended, could the anxiety of doubt, and meaninglessness, and guilt be taken into the courage to be (Tillich 1955: 76-77; Moore 2009; Ferguson 2010).

Mysticism

The God above God was the object of all mystical longing in East and West: even the mystical post-theism of the critical theorists of society as the result of the radical interpretation of the Biblical religion in terms of naturalism and humanism: the humanization of nature and the naturalization of man (Genesis 1, 2, 3. Scholem 1935; 1967; 1973b; 1977a; 1977b; 1977c; 1980; 1982; 1989; Buber 1937; 1952; 1957; 1960; 1965; 1966; 1987a; 1967b; 1968; 1970a; 1970b; 1970c; 1972; 1973a; 1973b; 1983; 1985; 1991a; 1991b; 1992; 1994; 1999b; 1999c; 2002a; 2002b; 2002c; 2002d; 2002e; 2003; Blakney 1941; Boehme 1938; 1962; 2005; Marx 2000; Horkheimer 1985g: chaps. 17, 29; 37; 40; Fromm 1950; 1966b; 1974; 1976; 1990b; 1999; 2001; Fromm/Suzuki/ Martino 1960; Benjamin 1950; 1955a; 1955c; 1968; 1977; 1978a; 1978b; 1996b; 1996c; 1997; Tillich 1926; 1929; 1933; 1948; 1951; 1952: 186-190; Moore 2009; Ferguson 2010). However, in Tillich's view, also Oriental and Occidental mysticism had to be concretely negated, in order to reach the God above God (Horkheimer/ Adorno 1969a; 1969b; 1972a 1972b; 1984; 2002; Buber 1937; 1952; 1957; 1960; 1965; 1966; 1987a; 1967b; 1968; 1970a; 1970b; 1970c; 1972; 1973a; 1973b; 1983; 1985; 1991a; 1991b; 1992; 1994; 1999b; 1999c; 2002a; 2002b; 2002c; 2002d; 2002e; 2003; Tillich 1926; 1929; 1933; 1948; 1951; 1952: 186-190 ; 1955: 76-77; Moore 2009; Ferguson 2010). Mysticism did not take seriously enough the concrete reality and the doubt concerning it. As mysticism plunged directly into the *Ground of being* and meaning, the totally Other, it left the concrete world of finite values and meanings behind. Therefore, mysticism did not solve the modern problem of meaninglessness. In terms of the present religious crisis situation in the West, this means that Oriental mysticism is not the solution of the problems of Occidental liberalism or existentialism. The God above the God of theism is not the devaluation of the meanings, which doubt has thrown into the abyss of meaninglessness in consequence of World War I, and fascism, and World War II and the wars in Vietnam, Iraq, Afghanistan, Libya, etc., and the approach of alternative Future I - the totally administered society:

he is rather their potential restitution (Hegel 1986c: 72; 1986r: 467; . 1986s: 362, 371; Flechtheim 1971; Horkheimer 1985g: chaps. 18; 19; 20; 21; 22; 25; 26; 30; 32; 34; 35; 36; 37; 40; Tillich 1952: 186-187; Moore 2009; Ferguson 2010). Nevertheless, in Tillich's view, radical and absolute faith agreed with the faith implied in mysticism in that both transcended the theistic objectivation of a God, who is a being. For mysticism such an objectified God was not more real than any finite being. For the courage to be such an objectified God has disappeared in the abyss of meaninglessness, with every other value and meaning connected with him (Scholem 1935; 1967; 1973b; 1977a; 1977b; 1977c; 1980; 1982; 1989; Buber 1952; 1960; 1991b; 1993; 1999b; 19999c; 2002a; 2002c; 2002e; Blakney 1941; Boehme 1938; 1962; 2005; Tillich 1952 186-187; Moore 2009; Ferguson 2010).

Dialectical Encounter

According to Tillich, the God above the God of theism is present, although hidden as *Deus absconditus*, in every divine-human encounter (Tillich 1952: 187; Moore 2009; Ferguson 2010). The three Abrahamic religions and the corresponding theologies were aware of the paradoxical or dialectical character of this encounter (Psalm 4; 22; 91; Hegel 1986q; Horkheimer 1985g:chap. 17; 29; 37; 40; Tillich 1952: 187; Zizek/Milbank 2008; Moore 2009; Ferguson 2010). They were aware, that if God encounters man, God is neither Object nor Subject, and is, therefore, above the antagonistic scheme into which theism has forced him, in spite of the second and third commandment of the Mosaic Law (Exodus 20; Horkheimer. / Adorno 2002; Tillich 1952: 187). They were aware, that individualism or personalism with respect to God were balanced by a transpersonal Presence of the Divine (Scholem 1935; 1967; 1973b; 1977a; 1977b; 1977c; 1980; 1982; 1989; Buber 1952; 1960; 1991b; 1993; 1999b; 1999c; 2002a; 2002c; 2002e; Blakney 1941; Boehme 1938;

1962; 2005; Tillich 1952: 187). They were' aware that the forgiveness of sins can be accepted only, if the power of acceptance is effective in man: Biblically speaking, if the power of grace is effective in man. The Abbot Andrew Marr, OSB, of St. Gregory's Abbey, Three Rivers, Michigan, speaks of the *strange and hidden ways grace works* in some people, who may have been effected without ever knowing (Marr 2011; Tillich 1952: 187; Moore 2009; Ferguson 2010). The Abrahamic religions were aware of the paradoxical or dialectical character of every prayer, of speaking to somebody, to whom man can not speak, because he is not *somebody*, of asking somebody, of whom man can not ask anything, because he gives or gives not before he is asked, of saying *thou* to somebody, who is nearer to the I than the I is to itself: shortly, he transcends and resolves the subject - object antagonism, which underlies all antagonisms in nature and history: Nicolas of Cusa spoke of the *Coincidentia oppositorum* (Scholem 1935; 1967; 1973b; 1977a; 1977b; 1977c; 1980; 1982; 1989; Buber 1952; 1960; 1991b; 1993; 1999b; 19999c; 2002a; 2002c; 2002e; Blakney 1941; Boehme 1938; 1962; 2005; Nicolas de Cusa 1962; Freud 1939; 1946; 1955; 1962a; 1962b; 1964; 1977; 1992; Fromm 1950; 1959; 1964; 1967; 1976; 1980b; 1992; 2001; Küng 1978; 1990a; Tillich 1952: 187; Zizek/Milbank 2008; Moore 2009; Ferguson 2010). Each of these paradoxes, or negations, or dialectics drives the religious consciousness toward a God above the God of theism (Zizek 2007; 2009; Zizek/Milbank 2008).

Participation and Individualization

In Tillich's view, the courage to be in the present late capitalistic world, which is rooted in the experience of the God above the God of theism, unites and transcends the courage to be as a part and the courage to be as oneself (Hegel 1986g; Tillich 1926; 1929; 1933; 1948; 1951; 1952: 186-190; Adorno 1961; 1952: 585-595; 1963; 1966; 1969a;

1969b; 1970a; 1973b; 1973d; 1973e; 1979; 1980a; 1980b; Fromm 1932a; 1932b; 1950; 1956; 1959; 1964; 1966a; 1966b; 1967; 1970b; 1972a; 1974; 1976). It avoids both extremes, the loss of oneself by participation in a fascist or socialist mass movement, and the loss of one's world by individualization in atomistic liberal civil society (Reich 1971; 1976; Tillich 1926; 1929; 1933; 1948; 1951; 1952: 186-190; Adorno 1961; 1952: 585-595; 1963; 1966; 1969a; 1969b; 1970a; 1973b; 1973d; 1973e; 1979; 1980a; 1980b; Fromm 1932a; 1932b; 1950; 1956; 1959; 1964; 1966a; 1966b; 1967; 1970b; 1972a; 1974; 1976; Moore 2009; Ferguson 2010). The acceptance of the God above the God of theism made people a part of that, which was not also a part, but is the ground of the whole. Therefore, peoples' self was not lost in a larger whole, which submerged it in the life of a limited group. If the self participated in the power of Being-itself, it received itself back (Thomas Aquinas 1922; Tillich 1926; 1929; 1933; 1948; 1951; 1952: 186-190; Adorno 1961; 1952: 585-595; 1963; 1966; 1969a; 1969b; 1970a; 1973b; 1973d; 1973e; 1979; 1980a; 1980b; Fromm 1932a; 1932b; 1950; 1956; 1959; 1964; 1966a; 1966b; 1967; 1970b; 1972a; 1974; 1976). That was so, because the power of Being acted through the power of the individual selves. It did not swallow them up as every limited whole, every collectivism, and every conformism does. (Adorno 1961; 1952: 585-595; 1963; 1966; 1969a; 1969b; 1970a; 1973b; 1973d; 1973e; 1979; 1980a; 1980b; Tillich 1926; 1929; 1933; 1948; 1951; 1952: 186-190; Moore 2009; Ferguson 2010).

The Church

In Tillich's view, this was, why the Church, which stood for the power of Being - itself or for the God, who determinately negates the God of the world-religions, claimed to be the mediator of the courage to be. in the late capitalist society (Thomas Aquinas 1922; Tillich 1926; 1929; 1933; 1948; 1951; 1952: 188; 1955a; 1955b; 1957; 1963a; 1963b;

1972; 1977; 1983; Küng 1970; 1972; 1976; 1978; 1990b; 1981a; 1991b; 1992; 1993a; 1993b; 1994a; 1994b; 2004; 2009; Küng/ Homolka 2009; Küng/Ess/Stietencron/Bechert 1984; Küng/ Kuschel 1993a; 1993b; Kuschel/Schlensog 2008; Baum 2004; 2009; Metz/ Wiesel 1993; Moore 2009; Ferguson 2010). However, so Tillich argued, a Church, - or for that matter a Synagogue or an Umma - which was based on the authority of the God of theism, entangled in the subject-object antagonism, could not make such a claim (Tillich 1926; 1929; 1933; 1948; 1951; 1952: 188; 1955a; 1955b; 1957; 1963a; 1963b; 1972; 1977; 1983; Küng 1970; 1972; 1976; 1978; 1990b; 1981a; 1991b; 1992; 1993a; 1993b; 1994a; 1994b; 2004; 2009; Küng/ Homolka 2009; Küng/ Ess/ Stietencron/ Bechert 1984; Küng/Kuschel 1993a; 1993b; Kuschel/Schlensog 2008; Baum 2004; 2009; Metz/ Wiesel 1993; Moore 2009; Ferguson 2010). It inescapably developed into collectivism itself (Tillich 1926; 1929; 1933; 1948; 1951; 1952: 188; 1955a; 1955b; 1957; 1963a; 1963b; 1972; 1977; 1983; Moore 2009; Ferguson 2010). But a Church, so Tillich argued, which raised itself in its message and its devotion and its *mimesis* to the God above the God of theism without sacrificing its concrete symbols - Creation, Christ, Eschaton - could mediate a courage to be, which could take into itself doubt, meaninglessness, guilt, and death. It would be the Church under the cross, which alone could do this, . It would be the Church, which preaches the crucified Jesus the Christ, who cried to God who remained his God after the God of confidence and providence had left him in the darkness of doubt and meaninglessness, and torture and death:

> And about the ninth hour Jesus cried with a loud voice:
> *Eli, Eli lamaha azavtani ?*
> (My God, my God, why hast thou forsaken me?)

(Psalm 22:1; Matthew 27: 46; Fromm 1966: 231-236; 1992; 2001; Tillich 1952: 186; Ferguson 2010). For Tillich, to be as a part in such a Church was to receive a courage to be, in which one could not lose one's self, and in which one received one's world.

Symbols

According to Tillich, a person could become aware of the God above the God of theism in the anxiety of guilt and condemnation, when the traditional symbols of the Abrahamic and other world religions, that had once enabled men to withstand the anxiety of guilt and condemnation, had lost their power in Modernity and in the transition to Post-Modernity (. Tillich 1926; 1929; 1933; 1948; 1951; 1952: 189-190; 1955a; 1955b; 1957; 1963a; 1963b; 1972; 1977; 1983; Horkheimer 1985g: chaps 17; 24; 25; 26; 27; 28; 29; 37; 40; Küng 1970; 1972; 1976; 1978; 1990b; 1981a; 1991b; 1992; 1993a; 1993b; 1994a; 1994b; 2004; 2009; Küng/ Homolka 2009; Küng/ Ess/ Stietencron/ Bechert 1984; Küng/Kuschel 1993a; 1993b; Kuschel/Schlensog 2008; Baum 2004; 2009; Metz/ Wiesel 1993; Flechtheim 1971; Tillich 1926; 1929; 1933; 1948; 1951; 1952: 188; 1955a; 1955b; 1957; 1963a; 1963b; 1972; 1977; 1983; Moore 2009; Ferguson 2010). When the symbol of *Divine Judgment*, which all three Abrahamic religions have in common, was interpreted by the Freudian enlightenment as a mere psychological complex, and *Forgiveness* as a remnant of the *father-image*, what once had been the power in those symbols could still be present and create the courage to be, in spite of the experience of an infinite gap between, what is the case in bourgeois or socialist society, and what ought to be (Freud 1939; 1946; 1955; 1962a; 1962b; 1964; 1969; 1977; 1992; Jung 1933; 1958; 1990; Drewermann 1989; 1992a; 1992b; 1992c; Tillich 1926; 1929; 1933; 1948; 1951; 1952: 189-190; 1955a; 1955b; 1957; 1963a; 1963b; 1972; 1977; 1983; Tillich 1926; 1929; 1933; 1948; 1951; 1952: 188; 1955a; 1955b; 1957; 1963a; 1963b; 1972; 1977; 1983; Moore 2009; Ferguson 2010). The Jewish,

Christian, or Islamic courage to be returned in post-theism, but not supported by the faith in a judging and forgiving God, as it had been the case in all forms of theism (Tillich 1926; 1929; 1933; 1948; 1951; 1952: 189-190; 1955a; 1955b; 1957; 1963a; 1963b; 1972; 1977; 1983; Küng 1991b; 1994a; 2004 Tillich 1926; 1929; 1933; 1948; 1951; 1952: 188; 1955a; 1955b; 1957; 1963a; 1963b; 1972; 1977; 1983). It returned in post-theism in terms of the radical and absolute faith, which says *Yes*, although there was no special power, that conquers guilt. The courage to take the anxiety of meaninglessness, guilt and death upon oneself, is the boundary line, up to which the courage to be can go (Tillich 1926; 1929; 1933; 1948; 1951; 1952: 189-190; 1955a; 1955b; 1957; 1963a; 1963b; 1972; 1977; 1983; Küng 1991b; 1994a; 2004; Habermas 1961; 1971; 1977; 1978a; 1978e; 1978d; 1982; 1986; 1988a; 1988b; 1990chap. 1; 1991a: part III; 1992c; 1999; 2001a; 2002; 2005; Tillich 1926; 1929; 1933; 1948; 1951; 1952: 188; 1955a; 1955b; 1957; 1963a; 1963b; 1972; 1977; 1983; Moore 2009; Ferguson 2010); Beyond it there was mere non-being, or nothingness (Hegel 1964; 1986c; Tillich 1926; 1929; 1933; 1948; 1951; 1952: 189-190; 1955a; 1955b; 1957; 1963a; 1963b; 1972; 1977; 1983; Küng 1991b; 1994a; 2004; Tillich 1926; 1929; 1933; 1948; 1951; 1952: 188; 1955a; 1955b; 1957; 1963a; 1963b; 1972; 1977; 1983; Moore 2009; Ferguson 2010). Within it all forms of courage were reestablished in the power of the God above the God of theism. For Tillich, the courage to be was rooted in the God, who appears, when the God of theism has disappeared in the anxiety of doubt., meaninglessness, guilt, and death in the context of late capitalist society (Adorno 1951; 1952: 585-595; 1969a; 1969b; 1970a; 1970b; 1973c; 1973d; 1973e; 1978; 1979; 1980a; 1980b; 1991a; 1994; 1995b; 1997h; 1997i-1; Tillich 1926; 1929; 1933; 1948; 1951; 1952: 189-190; 1955a; 1955b; 1957; 1963a; 1963b; 1972; 1977; 1983; Küng 1991b; 1994a; 2004; Moore 2009; Moore 2009; Ferguson 2010).

V. Solution to the Dichotomies

Tillich's friend, the analytical social psychologist and critical theorist Erich Fromm, interpreted with the help of Hegel, Marx, and Freud radically naturalistically-humanistically the Hebrew Bible and its traditions toward a post-theistic religiosity, concentrating throughout his life work on the notions of God, Man, History, Sin and Repentance, the Way-Halakha, and the Psalms, particularly Psalm 22, in the context of and in opposition to the more and more reified and commodified globalized late capitalistic society, moving toward alternative Future I - a necrophilous, totally mechanized, burocratized, computerized, and robotized technocratic society, and alternative Future II - an even more necrophilous, more and more militarized society, aiming at the collision of civilizations and corresponding ABC wars, and in support of tendencies toward alternative Future III - a biophilous society, characterized by a humanized technology, the sublimation of aggression, and a socialist humanism or humanist socialism (Hegel 1896; 1964; 1965; 1969; 1972; 1976; 1979; 1986a; 1986b; 1986c; 1986e; 1986f; 1986g; 1985p; 1986q; Marx 1871; 1906; 1951; 1953; 1956; 1961a; 1961b; 1961c; 1963; 1964; 1974; 1977; 2000; Marx/ Engels 1953a; 1953b; 1953c; 1955; 1960; 2005; Engels 1967; Freud 139; 1946; 1955; 1962a; 1962b; 1964; 1969; 1977; 1992; 1993; 1995a; 1995b; Horkheimer 1932; : 125-144; 1936; 1966' 1967a; 1970b; 1970c; 1971 1972; 1973; 1981a; 1981b; 1981c; 1985g: chaps. 17; 29; 37; 40; Adorno 1951; 1952; 1962; 1963; 1966; 1969a; 1969b; 1969c; 1970a; 1970b; 1973b 1974; 1979; 1980a; 1980b; 1991a; 1993b; 1993c; 1995b; 1997b; 1997c; 1997d; 1997f; 1997h; 1997i-1; 1997j-1; 1997u; Fromm 1932a; 1932b; 1950; 1957; 1959; 1961; 1964; 1966a; 1966b; 1966c; 1967; 1968; 1970a; 1970b; 1972a; 1972b; 1973; 1974; 1975; 1976; 1980a; 1980b; 1986; 1990a; 1990b; 1992; 1995; 1997; 1999; Fromm/ Suzuli/Martino 1960; Fromm/Xirau 1979; Funk 1995; 1999; 2000; Funk/Joach/Meyer 2000. ; Schmid-Noerr 2000: 7-40;

Mühlleitner 2000: 41-56; Bonss 2000: 57-82; Wolf 2000: 83-100; Flechtheim 1971; Flechtheim/Lohmann 2001 Thierse 2011: 20-23; Nida-Rümelin 2011: 23-25; Neian 2011: 48-51; Maas 2011: 51-54; Krell 2011: 77-80; Moore 2009; Ferguson 2010; Baron 2011: 65-68;Kesting 2011:68-70;Hochgeschwender 2010;Keegan 2010; MacPherson 2010;Lucke 2011:62-64). According to Fromm, the Jewish, Christian, and Islamic idea of the One God had expressed once in the evolution of religion a new answer for the solution of the religious and secular dichotomy as well as other antagonisms of human existence (Hegel 1986p; 1986q; Marx 2000; Fromm 1966 cap. Ii; Küng 1991b; 1994a; 2004; Moore 2009; Ferguson 2010). Man could find oneness with the world of nature and history, not by regressing to the pre-human state of evolution, but by the full development of his specifically human qualities: love and reason (Fromm 1956; 1959; 1966b:17-62; 1967; 1970b; 1974; 1976; 1980b; 1992; 1995; 1997; 1999; 2001, Moore 2009; Ferguson 2010). In Fromm's view, the worship of God was first of all the fight against and the concrete and determinate negation of idolatry (Exodus 20; Horkheimer/Adorno 20o2; Fromm 1966b:17-62; Lundgren 1998; Küng 1991b; Moore 2009; Ferguson 2010; Lucke 2011:62-64). On an earlier stage of religious evolution, the notion of God had been formed according to the economic, social, and political notions of a tribal chief or king (Psalms 93; 96, 97; 98; 99; 110; 145; Hegel 1986p; 1086q; Feuerbach 1904; 1957; 1996; Marx 1871; 1906; 1951; 1953; 1956; 1961a; 1961b; 1961c; 1963; 1964; 1974; 1977; 2000; Engels 1967; Marx/Engels Freud 1939; 1946; 1966b:17-62; Parsons 1964; 1965; 1971; Parsons/Shils 1951; Otto 1969; 1991; Fromm 1966b:17-62; Küng 1991b). In the next stage of religious evolution, the God-image had been developed according to a constitutional monarch, who was obligated to man, to abide by his own principles: love and justice (Psalm 93; 98; 99; Fromm 1966b:17-62; Nida-Rümelin 2011:23-25).

The Theos Agnotos

According to Fromm, in the next stage of religious evolution, this God became the *nameless God*: the *Theos Agnotos*, the God, about whom no attributes of essence could be predicated (Exodus 20; Acts 17; Hegel 1986q; Feuerbach 1904; 1957; 1996; Marx 2000; Engels 1967; Freud 1939; 1946; 1966b:17-62; Parsons 1964; 1965; 1971; Parsons/Shils 1951; Otto 1969; 1991; Horkheimer/Adorno 1969a; 1969b; 1972a; 2002; Fromm 1956; 1959; 1966b:17-62; 1967; 1970b; 1974; 1976; 1980b; 1992; 1995; 1997; 1999; 2001; Schmid-Noerr 2000: 7-40; Mühlleitner 2000: 41-56; Bonss 2000: 57-82; Wolf 2000: 83-100; Küng 1991b). This God without positive attributes was worshiped *in silence* (Blakney 1941; Fromm 17-62). This God had ceased to be an authoritarian God. Now man had to become fully independent. That meant, that man had to become autonomous even in relation to God (Horkheimer/Adorno 1969a; 1969b; 1972a; 2002; Fromm 1956; 1959; 1966b:17-62; 1967; 1970b; 1974; 1976; 1980b; 1992; 1995; 1997; 1999; 2001; Adorno/Kogon 1958a: 392-402; 1958b: 484 - 498; Habermas 1990:chap 1; 1991a: part III; Kogon 1967; 2003a; 2003b; Küng 1991b; 1994a; 2004). Man even argued and bargained with God concerning justice (Genesis 18; 19). Fromm found in *negative theology* as well as in mysticism the same revolutionary spirit of freedom, which characterized the God of the revolution against the ancient slaveholder society and state of Egypt, which is yearly remembered, celebrated, and hopefully practically imitated in Judaism, Christianity, and Islam: during Pass-over, and the Easterly Last Supper or Eucharist (Exodus 1-15; Matthew 5 -7, 26-28; Luke 6, 22-24; Scholem 1935; 1967; 1973b; 1977a; 1977b; 1977c; 1980; 1982; 1989; Buber 1952; 1960; 1991b; 1993; 1999b; 1999c; 2002a; 2002c; 2002e Blakney 1941; Boehme 1938; 1962; 2005; More 1895; 1901; 1963; Bloch 1960; 1970a; 1970b; 1972; 1975a; 1975b; 1975c; 1985b; 1985e; 2009; Bloch/ Reif 1978; Habermas 1969; 1970; 1976; 1977; 1978a; 1978c;

1978d; 1981b; 1982; 1986; 1987b; 1988a; 1988b; 1990 chap 1; 1991a; : part III; 1991c; 1992a; 1992b; 1992c; 2001a; 2001b; 2001c; 2002; 2004b; 2005; Metz 1959; 1965; 1967; 1969; 1970; 1972a; 1972b; 1973a; 1973b; 1973c; 1975b; 1977; 1978; 1980; 1981; 1995; 1997; 1998; Metz/Peters 1991; Metz/Wiesel 1993; Moltmann 1969; 1996; 2002a; Küng 1991b; 1994a; 1994b; 2004; Moore 2009; Ferguson 2010). Fromm could not express this revolutionary naturalistic-humanistic spirit better than by quoting Master Eckhart:

That I am a man
I have in common with all men,
That I see and hear
And eat and drink
I share with all animals.
But that I am I is exclusively mine,
And belongs to me
And to nobody else,
To no other man
Nor to an angel nor to God,
Except in as much as I am one with him.

(Exodus 1-15; Matthew 5-7, 26-28; Luke 6, 22-24; Blakney 1941; 233-247; Scholem 1935; 1967; 1973b; 1977a; 1977b; 1977c; 1980; 1982; 1989; Buber 1952; 1960; 1991b; 1993; 1999b; 19999c; 2002a; 2002c; 2002e; Boehme 1938; 1962; 2005; More 1895; 1901; 1963). In the perspective of the dialectical religiology, this mystical-political revolutionary spirit of Master Eckhart and Fromm is to be translated into the immediate context of the present macro-paradigmatic transition period between Modernity and Post-Modernity, which at this moment is characterized by an anti-utopian, anti-intellectual, neo-fascist or neo-liberal, conservative-revolutionary or, better still, counter-revolutionary mass-culture and culture industry in the service of a global corporate ruling class; and is to be practiced by masses of people, who are frustrated and angry, because in the catastrophic world-wide financial crisis of 2008-2011 etc, caused by anti-Keynesian, neo-conservative de-regulation and privatization since President Reagan, they have lost their jobs, their homes, their pensions, and who always were, or have been more recently politically disenfranchised; and is to be motivated and guided by thoughts derived from Moses, Jesus of Nazareth and Mohammed, from Hegel and Kant, and from Marx and Freud, against that what ought not to be, and thus is against God, in that what is the case in late bourgeois society: against alternative Future I - extreme capitalist exploitation and domination, against alternative Future II - one more and more aggressive conventional war after the other, and finally inter - civilizational ABC war, and toward alternative Future III - a global society of justice and peace and harmony (Exodus 1-15; Kant 1929; 1946; 1968; 1970; 1974a; 1974b; 1975; 1981; 1982; 1983; Hegel 1986g; 1986l; 1986q; Marx 1871; 1906; 1951; 1935; 1956; 1961a; 1961b; 1961c; 1963; 1964; 1974; 1977; 2000; Marx/Engels 1953a; 1953b; 1963c; 1955; 1960; 2005; ; Lenin 1972; Bloch 1960; 1970a; 1970b; 1971a; 1971b; 1972; 1975b; 1975c; 1985b; 1985e; 2009; ; Bloch/ Reif 1978; Fromm 1950; 1956; 1957; 1959; 1961; 1964; 1966a; 1966b; 1967; 1968; 1970a; 1971b; 1972a; 1972b; 1973; 1974; 1975; 1976; 1980a; 1980b; 1981; 1990a; 1990b; 1992; 1995; 1997; 1988; 2001; Mercieca 2011a: 1-6; 2011b: 1-5; Nida-Rümelin 2011: 23-25; Tillich 1926; 1929; 1933; 1948; 1951; 1952: 186-190; Neiman 2011: 48-51; Maas 2011: 51-54; Krell 2011: 77-80; Nida-Rümelin 2011: 23-25; Dannemann 2011: 70-73; Scheller 2011:64-67 Scheller 2011:64-67; Dannemann 2011: 70-73; Fuhr 2011: 67-70; Moore 2009; Ferguson 2010; Lucke 2011:62-64). In the perspective of the critical theory of society and religion, Fromm and the critical theorists are as little as Buddha, Moses, Kant or Marx *apostates* or god-less people: post- or non-theistic religiosity is not abstract atheism, and the *Theos agnotos*, the nameless God, is being unknown, nevertheless most real in and beyond nature and history (Exodus 20; Psalm 53. Acts 17; Kant 1929; 1946; 1968; 1970; 1974a; 1974b; 1975; 1981; 1982; 1983; Hegel 1986d: 448; 1986h: 161-162; 1985j: 380-381; 1986p: 57; 94; 99-100; 323; 1986q: 386; 1986r: 99; 148, 160; 376-377, 499; 1986t: 162-163; 194, 197, 288, 291, 318, 510; Horkheimer 1985g: chaps. 3; 13; 14; 15; 16; 17; 18; 22; 25, 26, 29; 30; 32; 34; 37; 40; 1985l: 286-287, 294-296, 467-492; 1987b: 15-74, 75-148, 237- 251, 295- 311, 1988d: chaps. 2; 5; 6; 7; 11; 12; Bloch 1960; 1970a; 1970b; 1971a; 1971b; 1972; 1978a; 1975b; 1975c; Fromm 1950; 1964; 1966a; 1966b; 1976; 2001; Habermas 1969; 1970; 1976; 1977; 1978a; 1978d; 1982; 1985b 1986; 1988a; 1988b; 1990: chap1; 1991a: Part III; 1992b; 1992c; 2001a; 2001b; 2002; 2004b; 2005; 2006a; 2006b; 2007; Habermas /Henrich 1974; Habermas/Ratzinger 2006; Sölle 1977; 1992; 1994; Sölle/ Habermas, etc. 1975; Sölle/Metz 1990; Küng 1970; 1978; Moore 2009; Ferguson 2010; Siebert 2010b).

X-Experience

While the Rabbis read in the Torah of Yahweh - *I am who I am*, or *I shall be who I shall be*, and while Hegel spoke of the *consciousness of the absolute Spirit* beyond the subjective and objective spirit, and while Marx de-mythologized, and de-ideologized, and de-ideologized, and defined religion as *sigh of the oppressed creature* against the oppressor, and as the *heart of a heartless world*, and remained silent about any reality beyond nature and history, and while Tillich taught about the *Ultimate Reality*, the *Ground of Being*, and while Altizer spoke of an *atheistic Christianity*, and Bonhoeffer of a *non-religious Christianity*; and while Adorno and Horkheimer announced the *longing for the totally Other* than the horror and terror of nature and history, which had once been called *Heaven*, or *Beauty*, or *Eternity*, Fromm explored the post- and non-theistic religiosity of the *X - Experience* (Genesis

1-10; Hegel 1986c; 1986p; 1986q; Tillich 1926; 1929; 1933; 1948; 1951; 1952; 1955a; 1955b; 1957; 1963a; 1963b; 1966; 1972; 1977; 1983; Fromm 1950; 1959; 1964; 1966a; 1966b: 57-62; 1968; 1970b; 1974; 1980b; 1990b; 1992; 1999; 2001; Fromm/ Suzuki/Martino 1960; Robinson 1963; Bultmann 1958; 1961; Bonhoeffer 1993; 2000; 2003; Küng 1970; 1978; 1990a; Schmid-Noerr 2000: 7-40; Mühlleitner 2000: 41-56; Bonss 2000: 57-82; Wolf 2000: 83-100). In his psychoanalytical- not theological - analysis of the X-Experience, Fromm identified, with the help of the Rabbis, Hegel, Marx, Freud and Tillich, its five main aspects or characteristic elements (Genesis 1 - 4; Exodus 20; Hegel 1986c; 1986p; 1986q; Marx 2000; Freud 1939; 1946; 1955; 1962a; 1962b; 1964; 1969; 1977; 1992; Tillich 1926; 1929; 1933; 1948; 1951; 1952; 1955a; 1955b; 1957; 1963a; 1963b; 1966; 1972; 1983). The first characteristic was, that people had experienced life as a problem: as a question, which needed an answer (Fromm 1950; 1959; 1964; 1966a; 1966b: 57-62; 1968; 1970b; 1974; 1980b; 1990b; 1992; 1999; 2001; Fromm/Suzuki/Martino 1960; Scheller 2011:64-67; Ferguson 2010). The non-X person, or the positivist, did not feel a deep disquiet about the existential and social, economic, and political dichotomies of life in modern civil society (Hegel 1986p; 1986q; Horkheimer 1974:101-104; 116-117; Adorno 1951; 1952; 1963; 1966; 1969a; 1969b; 1969c; 1970a; 1980a; 1980b; 1982; 1993c ; 1995b; 1997b; Marcuse 1960; 1961; 1962; 1965; 1967; Fromm 1950; 1959; 1964; 1966a; 1966b: 57-62; 1968; 1970b; 1974; 1980b; 1990b; 1992; 1999; 2001; Fromm/Suzuki/Martino 1960; Scheller 2011:64-67; Moore 2009; Ferguson 2010). For the non-X person life as such was not a problem. The positivist was not bothered by the global landscape of cries and tears, and feels no need for a theoretical or practical solution to the dramatic theodicy problem in its religious or secular forms (Leibniz 1996; Hegel 1986l 28, 549; 1986p:88; 1986s: 497; ; 1986t: 248; 455; Horkheimer 1971; 1985g: chaps 17, 29; 37; 40; Fromm 1966:

58; Metz 1995; Oelmüller 1990; 1992; Küng 1991b: 726-734; Scheller 2011:64-67; Moore 2009; Ferguson 2010). He is - at least consciously - satisfied with finding the meaning of life in the *status quo* of family, civil society, political state, international relations, or culture; in money or power, in sex, car, or career, or even - like Kierkegaard's aesthetical or ethical man - in acting in accordance with *his conscience*: *I did what I thought was right* (Hegel 1986c; 1986h; 1986i; 1986j; 1986m; 1986n; 1986o; Scheller 2011:64-67; Ferguson 2010; Lucke 2011:62-64). Hitler, the positivist, did precisely that (Hitler 1943; Horkheimer 1974:14, 101-104, 116-117; Moore 2009; Ferguson 2010). For the positivistic *metaphysics*, what ought to be has collapsed into what is the case in late capitalist society: what is, ought to be - even death. (Hegel 1986l; Heidegger 1956; 1968; 2001; Adorno 1932: 356- 378; 1951; 1952: 585 595; 1962; 1963; 1966; 1969a; 1969b; 1969c; 2070a; 1970b; 1973a; 1973b; 1973d; 1973e; 1974; 1979; 1980a; 1980b; 1992; 1993b; 1993c; 1995b; 1997b; 1997c; 1997d; 1997f: 413-523; 1997g; 1997h; 1997 I-1; 1997j-1; 1997j-2; Fromm 1951; 1961; 1970a; 1972b; 1973; Marcuse 1960; 1962; 1965; 1967; Habermas 1962; 1969; 1971; 1973; 1977; 1978c; 1978d; 1982; 1984a; 1984b; 1985; a; 1985b; 1987a; 1987d; 1988a; 1992b; 1992a; 2001a; Moore 2009; Ferguson 2010; Lucke 2011:62-64). To the mundane or secular positivist, life as it was, made sense. The non-X person did not feel the pain of his separateness from man and nature, nor the passionate wish and longing to overcome this separateness, and to find *at-one-ment* (Blakney 1941; Heidegger 1956; 1968; 2001; Adorno 1997f:451-452; Fromm 1966: chaps ii; iii; iv; v; vi; Scheller 2011:64-67; Moore 2009; Ferguson 2010).

Hierarchy of Values
According to Fromm, secondly for the X-experience there existed a definite hierarchy of values (Fromm 1966: 58-59). In this hierarchy the highest value was the optimal

development of man's own powers of reason, love, compassion and courage to be, and to resist, and to overcome non-being (Horkheimer 1985g: chaps. 17; 29; 37; 40; Fromm 1966b: 58-59; Tillich 1926; 1929; 1933; 1948; 1951; 1952; 1955a; 1955b; 1957; 1963a; 1963b; 1966; 1972; 1977; 1983; Schmid-Noerr 2000: 7-40; Mühlleitner 2000: 41-56; Bonss 2000: 57-82; Wolf 2000: 83-100; Moore 2009; Ferguson 2010). All religious and secular achievements were to be subordinated to these highest human spiritual or X-values. For Fromm, the hierarchy of values did imply Oriental and Occidental mysticism, but without asceticism. (Blakney 1941; 233-247; Scholem 1935; 1967; 1973b; 1977a; 1977b; 1977c; 1980; 1982; 1989; Buber 1952; 1960; 1991b; 1993; 1999b; 19999c; 2002a; 2002c; 2002e; Boehme 1938; 1962; 2005; More 1895; 1901; 1963; Fromm 1950; 1964; 1966a; 1966b: 58-59; 1970b; 1974; 1976; 1990b; 1992; 1997; 1999; 2001; Fromm/Suzuki/Martino 1960; Küng 1991b; 1994a; 2004). This hierarchy of values did not exclude secular pleasures and joys. It was not ascetic. The dialectical religiologist remembers, that neither Moses, nor Jesus of Nazareth, nor Mohammed was a mystical or an ascetic person (Exodus 2-5; Matthew 5-7; Luke 6; The Holy Qur'an 1934: Sura 1-10; Küng 1991b; 1994a; 2004; Bin Laden 2005; Byrd 2011). Through his hierarchy of values, Fromm tried - concretely superseding the idealistic models of Hegel, Schelling, Hölderlin, Goethe, Beethoven, and Mozart - to reconcile the secular and the religious consciousness, insofar as it made the secular life part of the spiritual life, and the secular life was permeated by the spiritual aims of the X-experience in the context of liberal civil society (Hegel 1972; 1979; 1986a; 1986b; 1986c; 1986p; 1986q; Fromm 1950; 1964; 1966a; 1966b: 58-59; 1970b; 1974; 1976; 1990b; 1992; 1997; 1999; 2001; Fromm/Suzuki/Martino 1960; 1970; 1981a; 1998; Habermas 1990: chap 1; 1991a: Part III; 992b; 2001a; 2002; 2004b; 2005; 2006a; 2006b; 2007; Habermas/Ratzinger

2006; Küng 1970; 1981a; 1998; Ashkenazy/Fabian 2009: 146-149; 150-151; 154-157; Moore 2009; Ferguson 2010).

Functional Rationality

In Fromm's view, closely related to the hierarchy of values was the third aspect of the X-experience: the concrete negation of the modern non-humanistic, merely instrumental rationality of means and purposes, aiming from its very start tangentially toward alternative Future I - the aggressive and necrophilous totally technocraticed and bureaucratized signal society (Horkheimer. 1932: 125-144; 1936; 1967b; 1970a; 1970b; 1970c; 1971; 1972; 1973; 1974a; 1974b; 1978; 1981a; 1981b; 1981c; 1985g: chaps, 34; 35; 36; 37; 40; 42; Fromm 1957; 1961; 1966: 58-59; 1970a: B 699-B705; 1972b; 1973; 1980a; 1990a; Marcuse 1960; 1961; 1965; 1967; Flechtheim 1971; Flechtheim/ Lohmann 2003; Schmid-Noerr 2000: 7-40; Mühlleitner 2000: 41-56; Bonss 2000: 57 – 82; Wolf 2000: 83- 1000)Moore 2009; Ferguson 2010; Lucke 2011:62-64). For the average person, so Fromm explained, particularly living in the non-dialectical - bourgeois - materialilistic culture of the modern commodity exchange society, life was a means toward ends other than the person himself or herself: these ends were money, power, pleasure, the production, distribution and consummation of commodities, etc. (Hegel 1986g; Marx 2000; Horkheimer. 1932: 125-144; 1936; 1967b; 1970a; 1970b; 1970c; 1971; 1972; 1973; 1974a; 1974b; 1978; 1981a; 1981b; 1981c; 1985g: chaps, 34; 35; 36; 37; 40; 42; . Fromm 1957; 1961; 1966: 58-59; 1970a: B 699-B705; 1972b; 1973; 1980a; 1990a; Marcuse 1960; 1961; 1965; 1967; Scheller 2011:64-67; Moore 2009; Ferguson 2010; Lucke 2011:62-64). If man in bourgeois society was not used by others for their needs and ends, he or she used himself or herself for his or her own (Fromm 1957; 1961; 1966: 58-59; 1970a: B 699-B705; 1972b; 1973; 1980a; 1990a; Scheller 2011:64-67; Moore 2009; Ferguson 2010). In both cases, he or she became a mere means. For the X person, man was an end, and never a means (Kant 1929; 1946; 1968; 1970; 1974a; 1974b; 1981; 1982; 1983; Horkheimer 1987b: 15-74; 75-148; 295- 311; Fromm1966: 58-59 Scheller 2011:64-67; Moore 2009; Ferguson 2010). Furthermore, the whole X - attitude toward life was one, in which each event, even the smallest one, was responded to from the standpoint of whether or not it helped to transform man in the direction of becoming more and more human (Fromm1966: 58-59; Baum1959; 1967; 1971; 1972; 1975a; 1975b; 1980a; 1980b; 1982; 1994; 1996; 2001; 2002; 2003; 2004; 2005; 2007; 2009; Baum (ed) 1999; Scheller 2011:64-67; Fromm 1957; 1961; 1966: 58-59; 1970a: B 699-B705; 1972b; 1973; 1980a; 1990a) . Whether it was art, literature, music, religion, philosophy or science, joy or sorrow, work or play, whatever happened was a stimulus to his or her becoming stronger and more sensitive (Blakney 1941; Hegel 1896; 1964; 1964; 1969; 1972; 1976; 1979; 1986a; 1986b; 1986c; 1986g; 1986i; 19896j' 1986l; 1986m; 1986n; 1986o; Adorno 1932: 356- 478; ; 1951; 1960: 643-653; 1962; 1963; 1966; 1969a; 1959b; 1969c; 1970b; 1873a; 1973b; 1973c; 1976g; 1980b; 1981; 1995a; 1996; 1997d; 1997g; 1997k; 1997l; 1997m; 1997n; 1997o; 1997p; 1997q; 1997r; 1997s; 1997u; Fromm1966: 58-59; Ashkenazy/Fabian 2010; Scheller 2011:64-67; Moore 2009; Ferguson 2010). For Fromm this process of constant inner metamorphosis and of becoming part of the world of nature and society and history in the act of living, was the aim toward which all other aims were subordinated (Schachtel 1959; Fromm1966: 58-59 Scheller 2011:64-67; Moore 2009; Ferguson 2010). Man was not a subject opposing the objective world, in order to transform it instrumentally and manipulatively for profit (Fromm1966: 58-59; Moore 2009; Ferguson 2010), Man was rather in the world, in order to make his being in it into the occasion for constant self-transformation. Therefore, the world was not merely an object standing opposite to him, but rather the *medium*, in which he discovered his own realty and that of the world ever more deeply. Also man was not a *subject*, the least indivisible part of human substance, an *a-tom*, in the Greek sense, and as such an *Ho Idiotaes*, or an *in-dividual* in the Latin sense. Man was not even Descartes' *Cogito ergo sum*, his lofty thinking subject, which dominated the modern history of philosophy and science and traditional theory up to the arrival of the critical theory, But man was a true *Self*, that was alive and strong precisely only to the degree to which *I* ceased to hold on to itself and was responding to the world (Hegel 1896; 1965; 1969; 1972; 1976; 1979; 1986a; 1986b; 1986c; Marx 1871; 1951; 1953; 1956; 1963; 1964; 1974; 2000; Freud 1939; 1946; 1962a; 1962b; 1964; 1969; 1977; 1992; 1993; 1995a; 1995b; Horkheimer 1985g: chaps 1, 2, 3, 4, 5, 7, 9, 11, 12; 13; 16; 17; 29; 37; 40; . 1987b: 15-148, 295- 311, 313-314, 319-320, 355, -357, 437, 438, 440-441-448-450; 1988a; 1988d: chaps 1; 2; 6; 7; 11; 13; 1987k: 13-69, 100-139, 289-344; Fromm1966: 58-59 ; Scheller 2011:64-67; Moore 2009; Ferguson 2010; Lucke 2011:62-64). In the perspective of the critical religiology, it would contradict not only Moses, the prophets, the Rabbis, the mystics, Hegel, Kant, Marx and Tillich, but also Fromm's own idology, that man on the top of the hierarchy of values would become for him another idol: another Golden Calf in the form of race, nation, or charismatic leader, or super-man (Exodus 20; Psalms 4; 46; 50; 73; 81; Ezekiel 22: 1-19; Lieber 2001: 709-712; Kant 1929; 1946; 1968; 1970; 1974a; 1974b; 1975; 1981; 1982; 1983; . Marx 2000; Horkheimer 1985g: chaps. 17, 29; 37; 40; 1988d: chaps. 1; 2; 5; 6; 7; Fromm 1950; 1956; 1957; 1961; 1964; 1966a; 1966b; 1967; 1970a; 1970b; 1972a; 1974; 1976; 1992; 1995; 1997; 1999; 2001; Neumann 1942; Scheller 2011:64-67; Moore 2009; Ferguson 2010; Lucke 2011:62-64). Fromm's X stands not for the world of nature or the world of man, society and history, but rather for the location before and beyond the system of finite life, nature and man, where once Hegel's Logic, his Logos theology, had been situated with all its categories and God - concepts from *Being* through *Essence* to the *Notion* and the absolute Idea (Hegel 1964; 1972; 1979; 1986a; 1986b; 1986c; 1986e; 1986f; 1986h; Fromm1966: 58-59; Scheller 2011:64-67; Moore 2009; Ferguson 2010).

X-Attitude

Fromm described the fourth characteristic element of the mystical X-experience, the *X-attitude,* as letting go of one's *Ego,* one's greed, and with it of one's fears and anxieties; a giving up of the wish to hold on to the *Ego,* as if it were an indestructible, separate entity; a making oneself empty, in order to be able to fill oneself with the natural and human world with all its negations and negativities, and to respond to its challenges, and to become one with it, and to love it (Blakney 1941; Scholem 1935; 1967; 1973b; 1977a; 1977c; 1980; 1982; 1989; Buber 1937; 1952; 1957; 1965; 1966; 1967a; 1967b; 1968; 1970a; 1970b; 1970c; 1972; 1973a; 1973b; 1985; 1991a; 1991b; 1994; 199b; 1999c; 2002a; 2002b; 2002e; 2002d; 2002e; 2003; Böhme 1938; 1962; 2005; Hegel 1986c:36, 39, 57, 74, 120, 123, 303, 427, 439, 533, 56 : 1986d:170, 434, 435, ; 1986e:49, 51, 86, 108; 118; 121, 122; 123; 124; 135; 140, 160; 165; . Freud 1939; 1946; 1962a; 1962b; 1964; 1969; 1977; 1992; 1993; 1995a; 1995b; Fromm 1950; 1956; 1957; 1961; 1964; 1966a; 1966b: 58-59; 1967; 1970a; 1970b; 1972a; 1974; 1976; 1992; 1995; 1997; 1999; 2001; Marcuse 1960; 1962; 1960a; 1970a: chap1; 1970b; 1973; 1975; 1979; 1980a; 1980b; 1984; 1987; 1995; 2001; 2005; Schmid-Noerr 2000: 7-40; Mühlleitner 2000: 41-56; Bonss 2000: 57-82; Wolf 2000: 83-100; Scheller 2011:64-67; Moore 2009; Ferguson 2010; Lucke 2011:62-64). For Fromm, as for Master Eckhart before, to make oneself empty did not express passivity, but rather *openness.* If one could not make oneself empty, one could not possibly respond to the world. One could not see, hear, feel, love, if one was filled with one's Ego; if one was driven by greed (Fromm1966b: 58-59; Moore 2009; Ferguson 2010). This kind of mystical X- attitude was quite different from the older one, which psychoanalysis had called *receptiveness* (Freud 1939; 1946; 1962a; 1962b; 1964; 1969; 1977; 1992; 1993; 1995a; 1995b; Fromm 1950; 1956; 1957; 1961; 1964; 1966a; 1966b: 58-59; 1967; 1970a; 1970b; 1972a; 1974; 1976; 1992; 1995; 1997; 1999; 2001; Moore 2009; Ferguson 2010). It had been passive. The emptiness of the X - attitude, however, was active: just as inhaling was as active as exhaling (Schachtel 1959; Fromm1966: 58-59). It was an active *transcending* of the *Ego* otherwise imprisoned in its environments (Hegel 1896; 1965; 1969; 1972; 1976; 1979; 1985a; 1986b; 1986c; 1986d; 1986g; 1986i; 1986j; 1986k; 1986l; 1986m; 1986n; 1986o; 1986p; 1986q; 1986r; 1986s; 1986t; Fromm 1932a; 1932b; 1950; 1956; 1959; 1964; 1966a; 1966b; 1967; 1968; 1970b; Habermas 1962; 1969; 1970; 1971; 1976; 1977; 1978d; 1978c; 1978d; 1979a; 1979b; 1981b; 1982; 1983; 1984a; 1984b; 1985a; 1985b; 1986; 1987a; 1987b; 1987c; 1987d; 1988a; 1988b; 1990chap. 1; 1991a: part III; Scheller 2011:64-67; Moore 2009; Ferguson 2010).

Naturalistic-Humanistic Transcendence

For Fromm, this active naturalistic-humanistic transcending into the immanence of nature as well as of man, society and history, constituted the fifth characteristic of the X-experience (Psalm 97; Hegel 1972; 1979; 1986a; 1986b; 1986c; Fromm 1950; 1956; 1957; 1961; 1964; 1966a; 1966b: 58-59; 1967; 1970a; 1970b; 1972a; 1974; 1976; 1992; 1995; 1997; 1999; 2001; Habermas 1990: chap I; 1991a:: Part III; Schmid-Noerr 2000: 7-40; Mühlleitner 2000: 41-56; Bonss 2000: 57 – 82; Wolf 2000: 83- 1000). But here again Fromm found the same problem as in the case of the word *religion* or *religious* in general. According to Fromm, *Transcendence* had traditionally and conventionally been used in the theistic sense of God's transcendence, not as a human phenomenon: i. e. as naturalistic-humanistic transcending. Fromm dealt, like Adorno, Horkheimer and Habermas before, with the transcending of the *Ego* and with, leaving the prison of its selfishness and separateness. In Fromm's view, whether people conceived of this transcendence as one toward God, or one into world-immanence was merely a matter of conceptualization. In psychoanalytical terms, the experience was *essential*, no matter whether it referred to God, or to the natural or human world, if it was understood theistically or post- and non-theistically. In Fromm's perspective, the mystical X-experience, whether theistic or post- and non-theistic, was characterized by the reduction, or even the disappearance of the *narcissism*, which dominates atomistic, liberal civil society (Horkheimer 1988d:chaps 1; 2; 6; 7; 8; 9; 11; 13; 17; Fromm 1964; 1966a; 1966b: 60-61; Scheller 2011:64-67; Moore 2009; Ferguson 2010). In order to be open to the world as nature and history, and to transcend his Ego, man had to be able at least to reduce, or better still completely to give up, his asocial or socio - pathological *narcissism*: or in other words, the pathological rationality, characterized by a merely ideological recognition, and permeating the familial, economic, political and cultural dimensions of the non-communitarian, socially and culturally torn - apart late capitalistic society (Horkheimer 1974: 62, 191-104, 116-117; Adorno 1951; 1952; : 585- 595; 1963; 1966; 1969a; 1969b; 1969c; 1970a; 1973b; 1973d; 1973e; 1976; 1979; 1980a; 1980b; 1980c; Fromm 1964; 1966a; 1966b: 60-61 ; Habermas 1961; 1975; 1977; 1978d; 1985b; 1987a; 1992c; 1995; 1998; 2001a; 2001c; 2003b; 2007; 2009; Honneth 1985; 1990; 1993; 1994; 1996a; 1996b; 2000; 2002a; 2004; 2007; Honneth/Joas 2002; Schmid-Noerr 2000: 7-40; Mühlleitner 2000: 41-56; Bonss 2000: 57-82; Wolf 2000: 83-100; Scheller 2011:64-67; Moore 2009; Ferguson 2010). Furthermore, man had to give up all forms of incestuous fixations, and of all that massive greed, which in the present global capitalistic crisis has reached a unique climax, as it was tending toward Post-Modern alternative Future I - the totally bureaucratized, technocratic society and Post-Modern alternative Future II - the most aggressive war society (Freud 1955; 1962a; 1962b; 1964; 1969; 1977; 1992; 1993; 1995a; 1995b; Fromm 1957; 1959; 1961; 1964; 1966a; 1966b: 60-61; 1967; 1970a; 1972a; 1972b; 1976; 1980a; 1980b; 1981; 1990a; 1990b; Scheller 2011:64-67 ; Schmid-Noerr 2000: 7-40; Mühlleitner 2000: 41-56; Bonss 2000: 57-82; Wolf 2000: 83-100; Moore 2009; Ferguson 2010; Baron 2011: 65-68; Kesting 2011:68-70;Hochgeschwender 2010;Keegan 2010; MacPherson 2010; Lucke 2011:62-64). Man had to overcome his destructiveness and his necrophilous tendencies trough creativity (Fromm 1957; 1959; 1961; 1964; 1966a; 1966b: 59-61; 1967; 1970a; 1972a; 1972b; 1973; 1976; 1990a; 1990b; 2001; 1966b: 59-61; Moore 2009; Ferguson 2010; Lucke 2011:62-64). Man had to be able, to be biophilous and to love life. Man had also to have a *criterion* for differentiating between a false X-experience, rooted in hysteria and other forms of mental illness - the syndrome of evil or decay, necrophilia or love of death, symbiotic, incestuous fixations and malignant narcissism: the non-pathological experience of love and union. (Freud 1955; 1962a; 1962b; 1964; 1969; 1977; 1992; 1993; 1995a; 1995b; Fromm 1957; 1959; 1961; 1964; 1966a; 1966b: 60-61; 1967; 1970a; 1972a; 1972b; 1976; 1980a; 1980b; 1981; 1990a; 1990b; Scheller 2011:64-67; Lucke 2011:62-64). Man must have a concept of true independence and autonomy (Fromm 1950; 1956; 1957; 1964; 1966a; 1966b: 60-61; 1967; 1968; 1970b; 1974; 1976; 1980a; 1980b; 1981; 1990b; 1992; 1999; 2001; Fromm (ed) 1966; Habermas 1986; Siebert 1987c; 2001; 2002a). Man had to be able, to differentiate between rational and irrational authority, between a true idea and an untrue ideology, between the willingness to suffer for his conviction and masochism (Hegel 1964; 1986c;

1986e; 1986f; 1986h; Freud 1955; 1962a; 1962b; 1964; 1969; 1977; 1992; 1993; 1995a; 1995b; Fromm 1957; 1959; 1961; 1964; 1966a; 1966b: 60-61; 1967; 1970a; 1972a; 1972b; 1976; 1980a; 1980b; 1981; 1990a; 1990b; Adorno 1970b; 1995b). The great Medieval Jewish thinker, Moses Maimonides, postulated physical and mental health as necessary requirement for the true prophet (Hegel 1896; 1965; 1969; 1986s: 515-516 518-519, 523-524; Fromm 1932b; 1950; 1956; 1957; 1959; 1964; 1966a; 1966b: 60-61; 1972a; 1972b; 1973; 1976; 1980a; 1980b; 1981; 1990a; 1990b; 1992; 20o1; Moore 2009; Ferguson 2010; Mercieca 2011c).

Naturalistic-Humanistic Religiosity

In Fromm's view, the so called *utopian* goal of alternative Future III - a rational and free, biophilous, and sane, and just society, characterized by the reconciliation of personal autonomy and universal solidarity, and by friendly and loving living-together, was more realistic than the *realism* and *pragmatism* of contemporary liberal and neo-liberal political leaders (Benjamin 1950; 1955a; 1955b; 1955c; 1968; 1971; 1072; 1974; 1977: caps 10, 11; 1978a; 1978c; 1978d; 1980; 1983a; 1983b; 1985; 1987; 1988; 1995a; 1995b; 1995c; 1996a; 1996b; 1996c; 1997/ Fromm 1956; 1957; 1959; 1961; 1964; 1966a; 1966b: 60-61; 1966c; 1967; 1970a; 1972a; 1972b; 1976: 201-202; 1980a; 1980b; 1981; 1990a; 1990b; 1995; 1997; 2001; Flechtheim 1971; Flechteim/Lohmann 2003; Marcuse 1960; 1962; 1965; 1967; 1969a; 1969b; 1970a; 1970b; 1973; 1975; 1979; 1980a; 1980b; 1984; 1987; 1995; 2001; 2005; Bloch 1960; 1970a; 1970b; 1971a; 1971b; 1972; 1975a; 1975b; 1975c; 1979; 1985a; 1985b; 1985e; 2009; Habermas 1969; 1970; 1971; 1973; 1978; 1977; 1978a; 1978c; 1978d; 1981b; 1982; 1983; 1984a; 1985b; 1986; 1987a; 1987b; 1987c; 1988a; 1988b; 1990; 1991a; 1991b; 1991c; 1997a; 1997b; 1998; 1999; 2001a; 2001b; 2001c; 2003a; 2903b; 2003c; 2004a; 2004b; 2004c; 2006d; Habermas/Bovenschen 1981; Thierse 2011: 20-23; Nida-

Rümelin 2011: 23-25; Neian 2011: 48-51; Maas 2011: 51-54; Schmid-Noerr 2000: 7-40; Mühlleitner 2000: 41-56; Bonss 2000: 57-82; Wolf 2000: 83-100; Moore 2009; Ferguson 2010; Mercieca 2011c ; Siebert 2010b). For Fromm, the realization of alternative Future III - the new society and the new man, was possible only, if the old motivations of profit, power and intellect., which dominate late capitalist society, were replaced by new ones, by being, sharing, understanding; if the marketing character was replaced by the productive, loving personality; if the authoritarian, cybernetic religion was superseded by a new radical naturalistic-humanistic religiosity (Marx 2000; Fromm 1976: 201-202; Scheller 2011:64-67; Moore 2009; Ferguson 2010; Mercieca 2011c; Siebert 1965; 1966; 1978; 1979a; 1979b; 1979c; 1979d; 1979e; 1985; 1986; 1987a; 1987b; 1987c; 1987d 1989; 1993; 1994a; 1994b; 1994c; 1994d; 1995; 2000; 2001; 2002a; 2002b; 2002c; 2003; 2004a; 2004b; 2004c; 2005a; 2005b; 2005c; 2010b). Those people, who were still authentically rooted in the theistic Abrahamic religions, may continue in their faith, hope and love, and all their good works (Fromm 1976: 201-2002; Küng 1970; 1972; 1976; 1978; 1980; 1981a; 1982; 1990a; 1990b; 1991a; 1991b; 1992; 1993a; 1994a; 1994b; 1998; 2004; 2009; Metz 1959; 1962; 1963; 1965; 1967; 1969; 1970; 1972a; 1972b; 1973a; 1973b; 1973c; 1975a; 1975b; 1977; 1978; 1980; 1981; 1984; 1995; 1997; 1998; Baum 1959; 1965; 1967; 1968; 1971; 1972; 1975a; 1975b; 1980a; 1980b; 1982; 1991; 1994; 1996; 2001; 202; 2003; 2004; 2005; 2007; 2009). However, those many people, who are no longer authentically rooted in the theistic or earlier world-religions, the crucial question was that of conversion to a naturalistic-humanistic religiosity without religion, without dogmas, without institutions, and without irrational authorities. Such naturalistic-humanistic *religiosity* had long been prepared by the movement of non-theistic religiosity from Buddha through Master Eckhart to Marx (Blakney 1941; Hegel

1986c; 1986g; 1986p; 1986q; Marx 1971; 1906; 1951; 1953; 1956; 2000; Bloch 1960; 1970a; 1970b; 1971a; 1985c; 1985d; 1985e; 2009; Fromm 1967; 1976: 201-202; 2001; Marcuse 1960; 1962; 1978 chap 1; Küng/Ess/Stietencron/Bechert 1984). People were not confronted in modern civil society with the choice between selfish bourgeois materialism - sex, car and carrier - and Ego - bound benefit calculations on one hand, and the Jewish, Christian or Islamic notion of God, on the other (Marx 1971; 1906; 1951; 1953; 1956; 2000; Küng 1991b; 1994a; 2004). In alternative Future III, secular social life itself - in all its aspects in family, civil society, constitutional state, history and culture, in work, leisure or personal relations, will be the expression of the religious spirit, and no separate institutional religion will be necessary any longer (Hegel 1896; 1965; 1969; 1972; 1976; 1979; 1986a; 1986b; 1986c; 1986d; 1986g; 1986j; Fromm 1967; 1976: 201-202; 2001; Horkheimer 1972 chaps. 2; 3; 4; 5; 6; 7; 1985l: 286-287, 294-296l 483-492). Positive religious elements will be rescued in secular form (Fromm 1967; 1976: 201-202; 2001; Habermas 1976; 1978a; 1978c; 1978d; 1982; 1984a; 1986; 1988a; 1990:ch. 1; 1992b; 1992c; 2001a; 2002; 2004b; 2005; 2006a; 2006b; 2007; Habermas/Ratzinger 2006), Fromm's demand for a new post - and non-theistic religiosity was in no way an attack on the existing theistic or other world-religions, be it Judaism, Christianity, Islam, Daoism, Hinduism, or Buddhism (Prabhupada 1974; Hegel 1986p; 1986q; Küng 1991b; 19994a; 2004; Küng/Ess/Stietencron/Bechert 1984; Fromm 1967; 1976: 201-202; 2001). It did, however, mean, that e. g. the Roman Catholic Church, beginning with the Roman bureaucracy, the Curia, had to convert itself to the spirit of the Gospels (Matthew 5-7; Luke 6; Acts 2: 42-47; 4:32-35; Fromm 1976: 201-2002; Küng 1970; 1972; 1976; 1978; 1980; 1981a; 1982; 1989. 1990a; 1990b; 1991a; 1991b; 1992; 1993a; 1994a; 1994b; 1998; 2004; 2009; Metz 1959; 1962; 1963; 1965; 1967; 1969; 1970; 1972a; 1972b;

1973a; 1973b; 1973c; 1975a; 1975b; 1977; 1978; 1980; 1981; 1984; 1995; 1997; 1998; Baum 1959; 1965; 1967; 1968; 1971; 1972; 1975a; 1975b; 1980a; 1980b; 1982; 1991; 1994; 1996; 2001; 202; 2003; 2004; 2005; 2007; 2009). It did not mean, that the so called socialist countries in Eastern Europe had to be de-socialized, as it then really happened through the victorious neo-liberal counter-revolution of 1989, but rather that their fake socialism, their so called *red fascism*, would be replaced by a genuine naturalistic-humanistic socialism (Marx 1971; 1906; 1951; 1953; 1956; 2000; Marcuse 1961; Bloch 1960; 1970a; 1971a; 1971b; 1972; 1975b; 1972; 1975b; 1975c; Fromm 1957; 1967; 1970b; 1976: 201-202; 1980a; 2001; Fromm (ed) 1966c; Habermas 1969; 1976. Moore 2009; Ferguson 2010; Mercieca 2011a; 2011b; 2011c; 2011d).

Meaning

In Adorno's perspective, already long before Auschwitz and Treblinka, the notion of meaning had become problematic in late capitalist society on its way to alternative Future I - total global economic and political administration, as *refugium* of the more and more fading theology (Hegel 1986 1896; 1964; 1965; 1969; 1972; 1976; 1979; 1986a; 1986c; 1986e; 1986f; 1986f; 1986g; 1986h; 1986j; 1986l; 1986m; 1986n; 1986o; 1986p; 186q; 1986r; 1986s; 1986t; Horkheimer 1985g:chaps 34; 35; 36; 37; 40; Adorno 1932; 1951; 1952; 1960; 1962; 1963; 1969c; 1970a; 1970b; 1973d; 1973e; 1979; 1997g:229-234; 1997u; Beckett 1970; 1972a; 1072b; Lucke 2011:62-64). Already before Auschwitz, Treblinka, Buchenwald, and Dachau it was in the face of the historical experience in late Modernity an affirmative lie to ascribe or attribute in any way a positive meaning to natural or human existence. That had consequences deep into the form and content of art, religion, and philosophy. While they have nothing any longer outside of themselves, which they could hold on to without ideology, so what they are missing can no longer be posited by any subjective act. The critical theory of society and the dialectical religiology contain like their poetical counterpart, the work of Samuel Beckett, a negative, inverse cipher - theology, which as it pushes beyond the mere abstract negation of meaning in globalizing antagonistic late capitalist society, concretely supersedes the traditional theological categories and extrapolates others out of nothing (Hegel 1986 1896; 1964; 1965; 1969; 1972; 1976; 1979; 1986a; 1986c; 1986e; 1986f; 1986f; 1986g; 1986h; 1986j; 1986l; 1986m; 1986n; 1986o; 1986p; 186q; 1986r; 1986s; 1986t; Adorno 1970b; 1997g:229-231; Beckett 1970; 1972a; 1072b). The theological turn-over, which happens in this process is, of course, not of the kind of a theology, which is happy already, when its issues are dealt with at all in modernity, no matter what judgment results, as if at the end of the tunnel of metaphysical meaninglessness the representation of the world as hell, the light of meaningfulness would shine into it again. In the view of the dialectical religiology, informed by Adorno, neither Becket nor the critical theorists must be affirmatively misunderstood and armed (, Anders 1956: 213-215; Adorno 1970b; 1997g:229-231; Beckett 1970; 1972a; 1072b; Lucke 2011:62-64; Siebert 2001; 2002a; 2011b). Beckett's works and the critical theory of society and dialectical religiology are absurd not through the absence of all meaning, in which case they would be irrelevant. They are rather absurd through the negotiations and proceedings about meaning. As the work of Beckett and of the critical theorists is dominated by the obsession of a positive nothing, so also by one of a developed and thereby, so to peak, deserved meaninglessness, which, however, could not be reclaimed as positive meaning. Today Beckett and the critical theorists do justice against all de-secularization attempts, through consequent determinate, concrete, specific negation of meaning, to the postulates of, and the longing for God, freedom and Immortality, or the totally Other, which once constituted the meaning of the works of great art, religion, and philosophy (Kant 1929; 1946; 1968; 1970; 1974a; 1974b; 1975; 1981; 1982; 1983; Hegel 1986 1896; 1964; 1965; 1969; 1972; 1976; 1979; 1986a; 1986c; 1986e; 1986f; 1986f; 1986g; 1986h; 1986j; 1986l; 1986m; 1986n; 1986o; 1986p; 186q; 1986r; 1986s; 1986t; Horkheimer 1985g: chaps 17, 29; 37; 40; Adorno 1932; 1951; 1952; 1960; 1962; 1963; 1969c; 1970a; 1970b; 1973d; 1973e; 1979; 1997g:229-231; 1997u; Beckett 1970; 1972a; 1072b; Karpov 2010: 232-270; Mercieca 2001a; 2001b; 2011c; 2011d; Siebert 2001; 2002a; 2011b). Modern literature as well as the critical theory participate through their highest representatives in the dialect that they as meaning connections, organized in themselves teleologically, express, that there is no meaning, and that they precisely, thereby, preserve in concrete, determinate negation the category of meaning: that precisely is, what makes their further interpretation possible and what demands it. (Hegel 1986 1896; 1964; 1965; 1969; 1972; 1976; 1979; 1986a; 1986c; 1986e; 1986f; 1986f; 1986g; 1986h; 1986j; 1986l; 1986m; 1986n; 1986o; 1986p; 186q; 1986r; 1986s; 1986t; Horkheimer 1985g:chaps 34; 35; 36; 37; 40; Adorno 1932; 1951; 1952; 1960; 1962; 1963; 1969c; 1970a; 1970b; 1973d; 1973e; 1979; 1997g:229-235; 1997u; Beckett 1970; 1972a; 1072b; Siebert 2010b).

From the City of God to the City of Progress

According to Fromm's dialectical view of history, later Medieval culture flourished, because people followed the vision of the *City of God* (Isaiah 11; 65; . 66; Revelation 21; 22; Augustine 1952; 1958; 1964; Thomas Aquinas 1922; Hegel 1896; 1964; 1965; 1969; 1976; 1985a; 1986b; 1986c; 1986e; 1986f; 1986g; 1986j; 1986l; 1986p; 1986q; 1986r; 1986s; 1986t; Fromm 1976:202), Modern civil society flourished, because people were motivated and energized by the vision of the growth of the earthly, secular *City of Progress* (Hegel 1986 g; 1986l; Fromm 1976:202) . In the 20th century - and the dialectical religiologist may add the beginning of the 21st century as well - this secular vision deteriorated to that of the *Tower of Babel*, which is now beginning to collapse and will ultimately – in Post-Modern alternative Future I – totally administered society, and Post-Modern alternative Future II - war society, bury everybody in its ruins (Genesis 11; Hegel 1986g; Marx/Engels 2005; Marcuse 1960; 1961; 1962; 1965; 1967; 1979; 1980a; 1987; 1995; 2001; 2005; Horkheimer 1932; 1936; 1967a; 1967b; 1970a; 1970b; 1970c; 1971; 1972; 1974a; 1974b; 1978; 1981a; 1981b; 1981c; 1985g: chaps. 34; 35; 36; 37; 40; 1987e; Adorno 1951; 1963; 1966; 1969a; 1969b; 1969c; 1970a; 1970b; 1973b; 1973d; 1973e; 1974; 1979; Flechtheim 1959: 625 - 634; 1962: 27-34; 1964: 148-151; 1966: 455-464; 1971; Flechtheim/Lohmann 2003; Fromm 1957; 1961; 1966b; 1970a; 1972a; 1972b; 1973; 1976:202; 1980; a; 1981; 2001; Honneth 1985; 1990; 1994; 1996a; 1996; b; 2000; 2002a; 2004; 2005; 2007; Moore 2009; Ferguson 2010; Mercieca 2011a; 2011b; 2011c; Scheller 2011: 64-67; Baron 2011: 65-68;Kesting 2011:68-70;Hochgeschwender 2010;Keegan 2010; MacPherson 2010; Lucke 2011:62-64). The fate of the Croatian City of Dubrovnik, once the competitor of Venice, situated south of the Island of Cordula, where the critical theorists of society met for discourse with the Zagreb Praxis Group as well as in the IUC Dubrovnik after World War II for several years, may be an example for the Babylonian self-destruction of capitalist society: Dubrovnik, where in the IUC we developed in the past 37 years our international course on the *Future of Religion* and our *dialectical religiology*, and in which we experienced the Yugoslav civil war from 1992 - 1997, which cost the lives of 200. 000 people, and the Serbian bombardment of the city, had survived not only Napoleon, but also the transition from Ustascha-fascism to self management socialism, and most recently from socialism to neo-liberalism, is now afraid of its total destruction, its death (Dragicevic, Oyen 2009; Dragicevic 2011). Daily up to twelve huge foreign ocean liners of different nations anchor in front of the city and thousands of visitors stream through the city day in and day out, and are told stories by tourist guides, which they can hardly understand because of the lack of historical consciousness and amnesia. The inhabitants of Dubrovnik cannot stand the continual stream of masses of foreigners, and therefore leave their homes. The City Commission is not able to limit the foreign ships to two a day, because of the city's hunger and greed for the maximalization of profit acquired after the victory of neo-liberalism and the destruction of the self-management system. The city which up to recently did not even allow advertisements in its walls, is destroying itself, because it can not curb collectively its suicidal greed. The City of Yalta, Crimea, Ukraine, where in February 1945 Roosevelt, Churchill and Stalin divided Germany, and Europe, and the world into a capitalist and socialist power realm up to the victorious neo-liberal counterrevolution of 1989,, and where since 11 years we have developed an international course on *Religion in Civil Society* and our critical theory of religion, suffers a similar fate as Dubrovnik: self-suffocation through the mania of unregulated, completely privatized, limitless profiteering and consequent financial and cultural crises. Dubrovnik and Yalta are symbols for the inner contradictions of global capitalism and for its downfall (Adorno 1932: 356-378; 1951; 1952; 1960; 1962; 1963; 1966; 1969a; 1969b; 1969c; 1970a; 1970b; 1973d; 1973e; 1974; 1979; Mercieca 20011a; 2011b; 2011c; 2011d; 2011e; Lucke 2011:62-64).

Toward the City of Being

If - so Fromm argued - the religious *City of God* and the secular *Earthly City of Progress* were *thesis* and *antithesis* in the sense of the Hegelian dialectical logic, then a new *synthesis* was the only alternative to the chaos and barbarism of alternative Future I and II: namely alternative Future III - the synthesis between the spiritual core of the Late Medieval World and the development of rational thought and science since the Renaissance (Hegel 1964; 1986c; 1986f; 1986g; 1986h; 1986j; 1986l Fromm 1957; 1961; 1966b; 1970a; 1972a; 1972b; 1973; 1976:202; 1980; a; 1981; 2001; Flechtheim 1959: 625 - 634; 1962: 27-34; 1964: 148- 151; 1966: 455-464; 1971; Flechtheim/Lohmann 2003; Dragicevic, Oyen. 2009; Dragicevic 2011; Baron 2011: 65-68;Kesting 2011:68-70;Hochgeschwender 2010;Keegan 2010; MacPherson 2010; Lucke 2011:62-64). Fromm called this alternative Future III, this synthesis, the *City of Being,* rather than of having, in which the City of God and the *City of Progress* would be determinately negated, i. e. criticized, as well as preserved, and elevated and fulfilled. (Isaiah 11; 65; . 66; Revelation 21; 22; Augustine 1952; 1958; 1964; Thomas Aquinas 1922; Hegel 1896; 1964; 1965; 1969; 1976; 1985a; 1986b; 1986c; 1986e; 1986f; 1986g; 1986j; 1986l; 1986p; 1986q; 1986r; 1986s; 1986t; Fromm 1976:202; Lucke 2011:62-64), Long before Fromm, Brother Eckhart of the Dominican Preaching Order, the Vicar of Thuringen, the Prior of Erfurt had spoken about this *being.* In his *Talks of Instruction* (Blackney 1941:Fromm 1950; 1956; 1957; 1959; 1961; 1966b; 1967; 1968; 1970a; 1970b; 1972a; 1974; 1975; 1976; 2001) Prior Eckhart instructed his spiritual children, the monks in the Dominican Monastery in Erfurt, Thuringen, as they sat together at Collation, that people ought not to consider so much, what they are to do as what they *are* : let them but *be good* and their ways and deeds will shine brightly. If you are just, your actions will be just too. Master Eckhart admonished his clerical audience, that they should not think, that saintliness came from occupation. Saintliness depended rather on what one *is*, the kind of work we did, did not make us holy, but we may make it holy. However *sacred* a calling may be, as it was a calling, it had no power to sanctify, : but rather as we *are*, and have the divine Being within. We blessed each task we did, be it eating, or sleeping, or watching or any other. Whatever people did who had not much of God's nature, they worked in vain., Thus, so Master Eckhart concluded his instruction on *being*, take care that your emphasize is laid on *being* good and not on the number or kind of thing to be done. The monks were rather to emphasize, the fundamentals on which their work depended: *being* rather than action, or having. (Blackney 1941:Fromm 1950; 1956; 1957; 1959; 1961; 1966b; 1967; 1968; 1970a; 1970b; 1972a; 1974; 1975; 1976; 2001; Mercieca 20011a; 2011b; 2011c; 2011d; 2011e; Lucke 2011:62-64; Siebert 2010b)

Alternative Futures

In the perspective of the dialectical religiology, while the Post-Modern alternative Futures I- the totally bureaucratized society, and the Post-Modern alternative Future II - the entirely militarized society are very undesirable, they are, nevertheless, also very possible and probable (Fromm 1976:202; Flechtheim 1959: 625 - 634; 1962: 27-34; 1964: 148-151; 1966: 455-464; 1971; Flechtheim/Lohmann 2003; Dragicevic, Oyen. 2009; Dragicevic 2011; Mercieca 20011a; 2011b; 2011c; 2011d; 2011e; Baron 2011: 65-68;Kesting 2011:68-70;Hochgeschwender 2010;Keegan 2010; MacPherson 2010; Lucke 2011:62-64). While Post-Modern alternative Future III - the truly democratic society, in which, universal solidarity and personal autonomy would be reconciled, is very desirable, it is, nevertheless, also very impossible and improbable, and hard discursively and institutionally to prepare and to achieve under present, late capitalist conditions (Hegel 1986a: 218; 1986 l: 107-115; 413, 418, 490-491; 513; 1986o: 352; 1986t:62; Horkheimer 1932; : 125-144; 1936; 1966; 1967a; 1967b; 1970a; 1970b; 1970c; 1971; 1972; 1973; 1974a; 1974b; 1978; 1981a; 1981b; 1981c; 1985g:

chaps 34; 35; 36; 37; 38; 39; 40; 42; 1987c; 1988a; 1991; Horkheimer/Adorno 1951: 284-291; 1969a; 1969b; 1972a; 1972b; 1984; 2002; Horkheimer/ Fromm/Marcuse 1936; Huntington 1996; 1998; Adorno 1951; 1952: 585-595; 1963; 1966; 1969a; 1969b; 1969c; 1969d; 1970a; 1970b; 1973b; 1975d; 1973e; 1979; 1980a; 1980b; 1980c; 1991a; 1993b; 1993c; 1994; 1995b; 1997c; 1997d; 1997f; 1997h; 1997i-1; 1997j-1; 1997i-2; 1997j-2; 1997o; 1997u; 1998a; 1998b; 1998c; 2000a; 2000b; 2000c; 2001a; 2001b; 2002d; 2003b; 2003d; Adorno/Dirks; 1974; Adorno/Kogon 1958a: 392- 403; 1958b: 484- 498; Fromm 1976:202; Flechtheim 1959: 625 - 634; 1962: 27-34; 1964: 148-151; 1966: 455-464; 1971; Flechtheim/Lohmann 2003; Dragicevic, Oyen. 2009; Dragicevic 2011; Schan/Busemer 2011: 4-8; Krell/Mörschel 2011: 25-29; Nonhoff 2011: 29-32; Siri 2011: 32-36; Grassi 2011:36-39; Stiegnitz 2011: 39-42; Hörisch 2011: 42-45; Zöpel 2011 45-48; Rulff 2011: 54-58; Thierse 2011: 20-23; Nida-Rümelin 2011: 23-25; Neian 2011: 48-51; Maas 2011: 51-54; Scheller 2011:64-67; Mercieca 20011a; 2011b; 2011c; 2011d; 2011e; Lucke 2011:62-64). In the view of the critical theorist of society and religion, it remains, nevertheless, the ethical demand, to resist or at least to transform Post-Modern alternative Future I - the totally mechanized, computerized, robotized, signal society; and under all circumstances to prevent Post-Modern alternative Future II - the complete war society, and to promote passionately Post-Modern alternative Future III - the City of Being, in which the antagonisms of late capitalist society would be overcome not only formal-, but rather also substantial - democratically, and in which man could fully realize his whole human potential in response to the world, and in which would be kept alive the longing and yearning for the One, whom the traditional believers still call Dao, Brahma. Nirvana, Ahuramazda, Elyon, Shaddai, Yahweh, Elohim, Adonai, Father, Allah, and which the traditional philosophers still name the *Good*, the *Gnosis Gnoseos*, the

Theos Agnotos, the *Absolute*, the *Unconditional*, the Notion including being, the Absolute Monad, the *Thing in itself*, the Transcendent, and which the critical theorists of society have concretely negated into the *X- experience*, or the *Non-Identical*, or the *Absolutely New*, or the *totally Other* than the finite, phenomenal world of the senses: with all its injustices, snares, terrors, arrows, weapons, plagues, illnesses, scourges, havocs, confusion, chaos, battles, wars, wicked people, disasters, catastrophes, severe storms, hurricanes, earthquakes, tsunamis, tornadoes, deadly devastations, hurts, troubles, lack of safety, insecurities, dishonor, aging and death, as well as predatory animals like lions, adders, sharks, killer whales, and crocodiles (Psalm 91; Anselm 1962; Blakney 1941; Kant 1929; 1946; 1968; 1970; 1974a; 1974b; 1975; 1981; 1982; 1983; Schelling 1860; 1946; 1977a; 1977b; 1993; Hegel 1986p; 1986q; 1986r; 1986s; 1986t; Benjamin 1955a; 1968; 1972; 1974; 1977: chaps 10; 11; 1978a; 1978c; 1978d; 1983a; 1983b; 1988; 1995b; 1995c; 1996c; Fromm 1950; 1956; 1964; 1966a; 1966b; 1970b; 1974; 1975: 200-202; 1990b; 1992; 1995; 1997; 1999; 2001; Fromm/ Suzuki/Martino 1960; Lundgren 19978; Horkheimer 1971; 1985g: chaps 17; 29; 37; 40; 1987i: 133-158, 172-180; 197-195; 196-242, 243-279, 459-466, 467-482; 1996s: 32-74; 2006; Adorno 1951; 1962; 1963; 1966; 169a; 1969b; 1969c; 1970b; 1973b; 1974; 1980b; 1993c; 1997b; 1997d; 1998a; 1998b; 1998c; 1998d; 2000b; 2000c; 2001b; 2001c; 2002a; 2002d; 2001c; ; 2003d; Adorno/Benjamin 1994; Adorno/Kogon 1958a: 392-402; 1958b: 484- 498; Fromm Ott 2001; 2004a; 2004b; 2004c; 2004d; 3005; 2006; Ott ed 2007; 2009; Schan/Busemer 2011: 4-8; Krell/Mörschel 2011: 25-29; Nonhoff 2011: 29-32; Siri 2011: 32-36; Grassi 2011:36-39; Stiegnitz 2011: 39-42; Hörisch 2011: 42-45; Zöpel 2011 45-48; Rulff 2011: 54-58; Thierse 2011: 20-23; Nida-Rümelin 2011: 23-25; Neian 2011: 48-51; Maas 2011: 51-54; Scheller 2011:64-67; Dannemann 2011: 70-73; Fuhr 2011: 67-70; Mercieca 20011a; 2011b; 2011c; 2011d; 2011e; Lucke 2011:62-64).

References

Adorno, Theodor W. 1932. "Zur gesellschaftlichen Lage der Musik. "*Zeitschrift für Sozialforschung.* 1:103–124, 356–378.

———. 1951. *Minima Moralia.* Frankfurt a. M. : Suhrkamp Verlag.

———. 1952. "Die Soziologen und die Wirklichkeit. Über den Stand der Sozialforschung in Deutschland" in *Frankfurter Hefte: Zeitschrift für Kultur und Politik,* (Aug.) 7&8:585–595

———. 1960. "Über Mahler, "*Frankfurter Hefte: Zeitschrift für Kultur und Politik.* 15 (9):643-653.

———. 1962. *Kierkegaard. Konstruktion des Ästetischen.* Frankfurt a. M. : Suhrkamp Verlag.

———. 1963. *Drei Studien zu Hegel.* Frankfurt a. M. : Suhrkamp Verlag.

———. 1966. *Negative Dialektik.* Frankfurt a. M. : Suhrkamp Verlag.

———. 1969a. *Dialektik der Aufklärung. Philosophische Fragmente.* Frankfurt a. M. : S. Fischer Verlag.

———. 1969b. *Drei Studien zu Hegel, Aspekte. Erfahrungsgehalt. Skoteinos oder Wie zu lesen sei.* Frankfurt a. M. : Suhrkamp Verlag.

———. 1969c. "Vernunft und Offenbarung, " *Stichworte, Kritische Modelle 2.* Frankfurt a. M. : Suhrkamp Verlag.

———. 1969d. *Stichworte.* Frankfurt a. M. : Suhrkamp Verlag

———. 1970a. *Der Positivismusstreit in der deutschen Soziologie,* Neuwied and Berlin: Hermann Luchterhand Verlag.

———. 1970b. *Über Walter Benjamin.* Frankfurt a. M. : Suhrkamp Verlag.

———. 1973a. *Äesthetische Theorie.* Frankfurt a. M. : Suhrkamp Verlag.

———. 1973b. *Negative Dialectic.* New York: The Seabury Press.

———. 1973c. *Philosophy of Modern Music.* New York: The Seabury Press.

———. 1973d. *Versuch, das Endspiel zu verstehen.* Frankfurt a. M. : Suhrkamp Verlag.

———. 1973e. *Zur Dialektik des Engagements.* Frankfurt a. M. : Suhrkamp Verlag.

———. 1974. *Kierkegaard. Konstruktion des Ästhetischen.* Frankfurt a. M. : Suhrkamp Verlag.

———. 1976. *Introduction to the Sociology of Music.* New York: The Seabury Press.

——. 1979. *Soziologische Schriften I*. Frankfurt a. M. : Suhrkamp Verlag.

——. 1980a. *Der Positivismusstreit in der deutschen Soziologie*. Darmstadt und Neuwied: Herman Luchterhand Verlag.

——. 1980b. *Minima Moralia: Reflexionen aus dem beschädigten Leben*. Frankfurt a. M: Suhrkamp Verlag.

——. 1980c. *Stichworte, Kritische Modelle 2*. Frankfurt a. M. : Suhrkamp Verlag.

——. 1981. *Noten zur Literatur*. Frankfurt a. M. : Suhrkamp Verlag.

——. 1982. *Philosophische Terminologie*. Frankfurt a. M. : Suhrkamp Verlag.

——. 1991a. *The Culture Industry: Selected Essays On Mass Culture*. London and New York: Routledge.

——. 1993b. *Einleitung in die Soziologie*. Frankfurt a. M. : Suhrkamp Verlag.

——. 1993c. *Hegel: Three Studies*. Translated by Shierry Weber Nicholsen. Cambridge, MA: The MIT Press.

——. 1994. *The Stars Down to Earth and Other Essays on the Irrational in Culture*. London: Routledge.

——. 1995b. *Studien zum autoritären Charakter*. Frankfurt a. M: Suhrkamp Verlag

——. 1997a. *Philosophische Frühschriften*. Frankfurt a. M: Suhrkamp Verlag.

——. 1997b. *Kierkegaard: Konstruktion des Aesthetischen*. Frankfurt a. M: Suhrkamp Verlag.

——. 1997c. *Dialectik des Aufklärung*. Frankfurt a. M. : Suhrkamp Verlag.

——. 1997d. *Minima Moralia*. Frankfurt a. M. : Suhrkamp Verlag.

——. 1997f. *Negative Dialectik*. Frankfurt a. M. : Suhrkamp Verlag.

——. 1997g. *Äesthetische Theorie*. Frankfurt a. M. : Suhrkamp Verlag.

——. 1997h. *Soziologische Schriften I*. Frankfurt a. M. : Suhrkamp Verlag.

——. 1997i-1. *Soziologische Schriften II*. Frankfurt a. M. : Suhrkamp Verlag.

——. 1997j-1. *Kulturkritik und Gesellschaft I*. Frankfurt a. M. : Suhrkamp Verlag.

——. 1997j-2. *Kulturkritik und Gesellschaft II*. Frankfurt a. M. : Suhrkamp Verlag.

——. 1997k. *Noten zur Literatur*. Frankfurt a. M. : Suhrkamp Verlag.

——. 1997l. *Philosophie der neuen Musik*. Frankfurt a. M. : Suhrkamp Verlag.

——. 1997m. *Die musikalischen Monographien*. Frankfurt a. M. : Suhrkamp Verlag.

——. 1997n. *Dissonanzen Einleitung in die Musiksoziologie*. Frankfurt a. M. : Suhrkamp Verlag.

——. 1997o. *Komposition für den Film. Der getreue Korrepetitor.* Frankfurt a. M. : Suhrkamp Verlag

——. 1997p. *Musikalische Schriften I-III*. Frankfurt a. M. : Suhrkamp Verlag.

——. 1997q. *Musikalische Schriften VI*. Frankfurt a. M. : Suhrkamp Verlag.

——. 1997r. *Musikalische Schriften V*. Frankfurt a. M. : Suhrkamp Verlag.

——. 1997s. *Musikalische Schriften VI*. Frankfurt a. M. : Suhrkamp Verlag.

——. 1997u. *Ob nach Auschwitz noch sich leben lasse: Ein philosophisches Lesebuch*. Frankfurt a. M. : Suhrkamp Verlag.

——. 1998a. "Das Problem des Idealismus. Stichworte zur Vorlesung 1953/54, " *Frankfurter Adorno Blätter*, 5. Munich.

——. 1998b. "Geschichtsphilosophischer Exkurs zur Odyssee. Frühe Fassungen von Odysseus oder Mythos und Aufklärung, " *Frankfurter Adorno Blätter,* 5. Munich.

——. 1998c. *Metaphysik. Begriff und Probleme*. Frankfurt a. M. : Suhrkamp Verlag.

——. 1998d. "Um Benjamin's Werk. Briefe an Gershom Scholem 1838-1955, " in *Frankfurter Adorno Blätter V*, Munich.

——. 2000a. *Introduction to Sociology*. Stanford: Stanford University Press.

——. 2000b. *Problems of Moral Philosophy*. Stanford: California: Stanford University Press.

——. 2000c. *Metaphysics. Concept and Problems*. Stanford, California: Stanford University Press .

——. 2001a. *The Culture Industry*. London: Routledge.

——. 2001b. *Zur Lehre von der Geschichte und von der Freiheit*. Frankfurt a. M. : Suhrkamp Verlag.

——. 2001c. *Kant's Criqtique of Pure Reason*. Stanford, California: Stanford University Press

——. 2002a. *Ontologie und Dialektik*. Frankfurt a. M. : Suhrkamp Verlag.

——. 2002b. *Quasi una Fantasia: Essays on Modern Music*. London. New York: Verso.

——. 2002c. *Essays on Music*. Berkeley: University of California Press.

——. 2002d. *Dialectic of Enlightenment: Philosophical Fragments*. Stanford, CA: Stanford University Press.

——. 2003b. "Konferenz: Dialektik der Freiheit" in *Mitteilungen des Instituts für Sozialforschung*, 14 (4):168-171.

——. 2003d. *Vorlesungen über Negative Dialektik*. Frankfurt a. M. : Suhrkamp Verlag.

Adorno, Theodor W., et al. 1976. *The Positivist Dispute in German Sociology*. Trans. by Glyn Adey and David Frisby. New York: Harper and Row.

Adorno, Theodor W. et al. 2007. *Aesthetics and Politics*. London:Verso.

Adorno, Theodor W. and Walter Benjamin. 1994. *Briefwechsel 1928-1940*. Frankfurt a. M. : Suhrkamp Verlag.

Adorno, Theodor W. and Walter Dirks [eds.] 1974. *Sociologica I. Aufsätze. Max Horkheimer zum Sechzigsten Geburtstag gwidmet*. Frankfurt a. M. : Europäische Verlag.

Adorno, Theodor W. and Karl Kereenyi. 1998. "Mythologie und Aufklärung. Ein Rundfunksgespräch in *Frankfurter Adorno Plätter* 5:89-104. München.

Adorno, Theodor W. and Eugen Kogon. 1958a. "Offenbarung oder autonome Vernunft. " *Frankfurter Hefte: Zeitschrift für Kultur und Politik*, 13 (Juni 6):392–402.

——. 1958b "Offenbarung oder autonome Vernunft. " *Frankfurter Hefte: Zeitschrift für Kultur und Politik*, 13 (Juni 7):484- 498.

Adorno, Theodor W., Else Frenkel–Brunswick, Daniel J. Levinson, and R. Nevitt Sanford. 1950. *The Authoritarian Personality*. New York: Harper & Row, Publishers.

Adorno, Theodor W. / Siegfried Kracauer. 2008. *Briefwechsel 1923-1966*. Hg. von Wolfgang Schopf. Frankfurt a. M. : Suhrkamp Verlag.

AngrickAndrej/Peter Jlein. 2011. " *Final Solution*" in *Riga:Exploitation and Annihilation 1941-1944*. Berghahn

Anselm, Saint. 1962. *Basic Writings. Proslogium. Monologium. Gaunilon's: On Behalf of the Fool.* Cur Desu Homo, La Salle, Illinois: Open Court Publishing Company.

Apel, Karl–Otto. 1975. *Der Denkweg von Charles S, Peirce. Eine Einführung in den Amerikianischen Pragmatismus.* Frankfurt a. M. : Suhrkamp Verlag.

———. 1976a. *Transformation der Philosophie. Band 1 Sprachanalytik, Semiotik, Hermeneutik.* Frankfurt a. M. : Suhrkamp Verlag.

———. 1976b. *Transformation der Philosophie. Band 2. Das Apriori der Kommunikationsgemeinschaft.* Frankfurt a. M. : Suhrkamp Verlag.

———. 1982. *Sprachpragmatik und Philosophie.* Frankfurt a. M. : Suhrkamp Verlag.

———. 1990. *Diskurs und Verantwortung. Das Problem des Übergangs zur postkonventionellen Moral.* Frankfurt a. M. : Suhrkamp Verlag.

Arens, Edmund. 1995. *Anerkennung der Anderen. Eine theologische Grunddimension interkultureller Kommunikation.* Freiburg, Basel: Herder Verlag.

———. 1997. *Kommunikatives Handeln und Christlicher Glaube, Ein theologischer Diskurs mit Jürgen Habermas.* Paderborn: Ferdinand Schöningh.

———. 2007. *Gottesverständigung. Eine kommunikative Religionsthiologie.* Freiburg: Herder.

———. 2009. "Alt, aber nicht fromm, " in *Herder Korrespondenz* 63/ 2:79-83.

Arens, Edmund, O. John, and R. Rottländer. 1991. *Erinnerung, Befreiung, Solidarität, Benjamin, Marcuse, Habermas und die politische Theologie.* Dusseldorf: Patmos Verlag.

Augustine, Saint. 1952. *The Confessions.* New York: Pocket Books, Inc.

———. 1958. *The City of God,* with an introduction by Thomas Merton. New York: The Modern   Library.

———. 1984. *Augustine of Hippo: Selected Writings.* Translated by Mary T. Clark. Glen Rock, NJ: Paulist Press.

Baldwin, Neil, 2001. Henry *Ford and the Jews. The Mass Production of Hate.* New York : Public Affairs.

Ashkenazy, Vladimir/Dorottya Fabian, 2010. *All of Music. The Life and Times of the Great Composers. 1. 000 Years of Classical Music* Elanora Heights, Australia: Millenium House.

Augustine, Saint. 1952. *The Confessions.* New York: Pocket Books, Inc.

——. 1958. *The City of God,* with an introduction by Thomas Merton. New York: The Modern Library.

——. 1984. *Augustine of Hippo: Selected Writings.* Translated by Mary T. Clark. Glen Rock, NJ: Paulist Press.

Baron,Ulrich.2011."Sieg der Zentralgewalt. Neue Bücher zum Amerikanischen Bürgerkrieg," In *Neue Gesellschaft/ Frankfurter Hefte* 6/58: 65-68.

Baudelaire, Charles. 1982. *Die Blumen des Bösen.* München: Diogenes Taschenbuch Verlag.

Baum, Gregory. 1959. *Is the New Testament Anti–Semitic? A Re-examination of the New Testament.* Glen Rock, NJ: Deus Books, Paulist Press.

——. 1965. *Catholic Quest for Christian Unity.* Glen Rock, NJ: Deus Books, Paulist Press.

——. 1967. *The Future of Belief: Debate.* New York: Herder and Herder.

——. 1968. *The Credibility of the Church Today: A Reply to Charles Davis.* New York: Herder and Herder.

——. 1971. *Man Becoming: God in Secular Experience.* New York: Herder and Herder.

——. 1972. *New Horizons: Theological Essays.* New York: Paulist Press.

——. 1975a. *Journeys: The Impact of Personal Experience on Religious Thought.* New York: Paulist Press.

——. 1975b. *Religion and Alienation: A Theological Reading of Sociology.*. New York: Paulist Press.

——. 1980a. *Sociology and Human Destiny.* New York: The Seabury Press.

——. 1980b. *Work and Religion.* New York: The Seabury Press.

——. 1982. *The Priority of Labor: A Commentary on Laborem Exercens– Encyclical Letter of Pope John Paul II.* New York: Paulist Press International.

——. 1991. *The Church in Quebec.* Ottawa: Saint Paul University, Novalis.

——. 1994. *Essays in Critical Theology*, Kansas City: Sheed and Ward .

——. 1996. *The Church for Others, Protestant Theology in Communist East Germany*, Grand Rapids, MI: Eerdmans Publishing Company.

——. 2001. *Nationalism, Religion and Ethics*. Montreal and Kingston. London. Ithaca: McGill–Queen's University Press.

——. 2002. "Public Letter of Gregory Baum to Lothar Beyer, " Le devoir, Montreal.

——. 2003. "Jewish–Christian Dialogue under the Shadow of the Israeli–Palestinian Conflict. " *Théologique*, 11 (1–2):205–221.

——. 2004. "Western Islam According to Tariq Ramadan. " *The Ecumenist: A Journal of Theology, Culture and Society.*

——. 2005. *Amazing Church: A Catholic Theologian Remembers a Half-Century of Change*. Maryknoll, New York: Orbis Books.

——. 2007. *Reading the Signs: Religious Pluralism and Economic Injustice*. Ottawa, Canada: Novalis.

——. 2009. *The Theology of Tariq Ramada: A Catholic Perspective.* Toronto, Ontario, Canada: Novalis Publishing Inc.

Baum, Gregory [ed.] 1999. *The Twentieth Century: A Theological Overview*. Maryknoll, NY: Orbis Books.

Beckett, Samuel. 1970. *Endspiel*. Frankfurt a. M. : Suhrkamp Verlag.

——. 1972a. *Warten auf Godot*. Frankfurt a. M. : Suhrkamp Verlag.

——. 1972b. *Watt*. Frankfurt a. M. : Suhrkamp Verlag.

Benedict XVI. 2011. *Great Christian Thinkers. From the Early Church through the Middle Ages*. Augsburg:Fortress Press.

Benjamin, Walter. 1950. *Schriften I*. Frankfurt a. M. : Suhrkamp Verlag.

——. 1955a. "Priviligiertes Denken. Zu Theodor Haecker's. Vergil (1932)" in *W. Benjamin, Gesammelte Werke*. Frankfurt a. M. : Suhrkamp Verlag.

——. 1955b. *Einbahnstrasse*. Frankfurt a. M. : Suhrkamp Verlag.

——. 1955c. *Schriften*. Frankfurt a. M. : Suhrkamp Verlag.

——. 1968. *Illuminations*. New York: Schocken Books.

——. 1971. *Drei Hörmodelle*. Frankfurt a. M. : Suhrkamp Verlag.

——. 1972. *Goethes Wahlverwandtschaften*. Frankfurt a. M: Suhrkamp Verlag.

——. 1974. *Charles, Baudelaire, Ein Lyriker des Hochkapitalismus.* Frankfurt a. M. : Suhrkamp Verlag.

——. 1977. *Illuminationen. Ausgewählte Schriften.* Frankfurt a. M. : Suhrkamp Verlag.

——. 1978a. *Ursprung des deutschen Trauerspiels.* Frankfurt a. M: Suhrkamp Verlag.

——. 1978b. *Briefe 2. Herausgegeben und mit Anmerkungen verstehen von Gershom Scholem und Theordor W. Adorno.* Frankfurt a. M. : Suhrkamp Verlag.

——. 1978c. *Versuche über Brecht.* Frankfurt a. M. : Suhrkamp Verlag.

——. 1978d. *Zur Kritik der Gewalt, und andere Aufsätze, Mit einem Nachwort von Herbert Marcuse.* Frankfurt a. M. : Suhrkamp Verlag.

——. 1980. *Moskauer Tagebuch: Mit einem Vorwort von Gershom, Scholem.* Frankfurt a. M. : Suhrkamp Verlag.

——. 1983a. *Das Passagen–Werk. Herausgegegeben von Rolf Tiedemann. Erster Band.* Frankfurt a. M. : Suhrkamp Verlag.

——. 1983b. *Das Passagen Werk. Herausgegeben von Rolf Tiedemann. Zweiter Band* Frankfurt a. M. : Suhrkamp Verlag.

——. 1985. *Aufklärung für Kinder. Rundfunkvorträge.* Frankfurt a. M. : Suhrkamp Verlag.

——. 1987. *Berliner Kindheit um Neunzehnhundert.* Frankfurt a. M. : Suhrkamp Verlag.

——. 1988. *Angelus Novus. Ausgewählte Schriften 2.* Frankfurt a. M. : Suhrkamp Verlag.

——. 1995a. "Paris, 24. Januar 1939. Ein Literaturbrief" in *Frankfurter Adorno Blätter*, 4.

——. 1995b. "Notizen zu einer Arbeit über die Kategorie der Gerechtigkeit. Mit einem Kommentar von Hermann Schweppenhäuser" in *Frankfurter Adorno Blätter*, 4:41–51.

——. 1995c. "Neue Baudelairiana. Un veröffentlichte Fragmente zur einer Neufassung des Flaneurs. Mit einer Notiz von Rolf Tiedemann" in *Frankfurter Adorno Blätter*, 4.

——. 1996a. *Das Kunstwerk im Zeitalter seiner technischen Reproduzierbarkeit.* Frankfurt a. M. : Suhrkamp Verlag.

——. 1996b. *Gesammelte Briefe. Band II. 1919 – 1924.* Frankfurt a. M. Suhrkamp Verlag

——. 1996c. *Ein Lesebuch.* Frankfurt a. M. : Suhrkamp Verlag.

——. 1997. *Gesammelte Briefe. Band III. 1925 – 1930.* Frankfurt a. M. : Suhrkamp Verlag. Berrigan, Daniel. 1972. *America is*

Hard to Find: Notes from the Underground and Letters from Danbury Prison. Garden City, NY: Doubleday and Company.

———. 1978. *Uncommon Prayer: A Book of Psalms.* New York: The Seabury Press.

———. 1989. *Isaiah, Spirit of Courage, Gift of Tears.* Minneapolis: Fortress Press.

Bin Laden, Osama. 2005. *Messages to the World. The Statements of Osama Bin Laden.* London: Verso.

Blakney, Raymond, B. 1941. *Meister Eckhart: A Modern Translation.* New York: Harper Brothers Publishers.

Bloch, Ernst. 1960. *Thomas Münzer: Als Theologe der Revolution.* Frankfurt a. M. : Suhrkamp Verlag.

———. 1970a. *A Philosophy of the Future.* New York: Herder and Herder.

———. 1970b. *Man on his Own: Essays on the Philosophy of Religion.* New York: Herder and   Herder.

———. 1971a. *On Karl Marx.* New York: Herder and Herder.

———. 1971b. *Im Christentum steckt die Revolte.* Zürich : Verlag der Arche

———. 1972. *Atheism in Christianity: the Religion of the Exodus and the Kingdom.* Translated by J. T. Swann, New York: Herder and Herder.

———. 1975a. *Experimentum Mundi, Frage, Kategorien des Herausbringens, Praxis.* Frankfurt a. M. : Suhrkamp Verlag.

———. 1975b. *Geist der Utopie.* Frankfurt a. M. : Suhrkamp Verlag.

———. 1975c. *Über Methode und System bei Hegel.* Frankfurt a. M. : Suhrkamp Verlag.

———. 1979. *Tübinger Einleitung in die Philosophie.* Frankfurt a. M. : Suhrkamp Verlag.

———. 1985a. *Erbschaft dieser Zeit, Erweiterte Ausgabe.* Frankfurt a. M. : Suhrkamp Verlag.

———. 1985b. *Naturrecht und menschliche Würde.* Frankfurt a. M; Suhrkamp Verlag.

———. 1985c. *Das Prinzip Hoffnung.* Frankfurt a. M: Suhrkamp Verlag. Vol. I.

———. 1985d. *Das Prinzip Hoffnung.* Frankfurt a/M: Suhrkamp Verlag. Vol. II

———. 1985e. *Das Prinzip Hoffnung.* Frankfurt a. M: Suhrkamp Verlag. Vol. III

———. 2009. *Atheism in Christianity*. London:Verso

Bloch, Karola, and Adelbert Reif. 1978. *Denken heisst Überschreiten: In Memoriam Ernst Bloch 1885–1977*. Köln. Frankfurt a. M. : Europäische Verlag.

Böhme, Jacob. 1938. *Schriften*. Leipzig

———. 1962. *Dialogues on the Supersensual Life*. New York: Frederick Ungar Publishing Co.

———. 2005. *Aurora*. Whitefish, Mt. : Kessinger Publishing Co.

Boer, Roland. 2010"Kairos and Akairos" in *Religion and Civil Society Materials of the VI International Seminar November in Yalta*, Tatyana A. Senyushkina [ed.] Simferopol: Tauria.

Boff, Leonardo. 1985. *Kirche, Charisma und Macht*. Düsseldorf: Patmos Verlag.

Bonhoeffer, Dietrich. 1993. *Mensch hinter Mauern. Theologie und Spiritualiät in den Gefängnisjahren*. Giessen/BaselBrunnen Verlag.

———, 2000. *Agent of Grace*, DVD. Directed by Eric Till, 2000. Berlin: NFP Teleart Berlin.

———, 2003. *Pastor, Pacifist, Nazi Resister*, DVD. Directed by Martin Doblmeier, 2003. New York: First Run Features. Bonss, Wolfgang. 2000. "Erich Fromms analytische Sozialpsychologie. Ein Konzept und seine Folgen. " in the *Institut für Sozialforschung. An der Johann Wolfgang Goethe-Universität*. Frankfurt am Main. *Mitteilungen*. Heft 11. September

Brecht, Bertolt. 1961. *Seven Plays*. New York: Groves Press Inc.

———. 1964. *The Three Penny Opera*. New York: Grove Press.

———. 1966. *Galileo. A Play*. New York: Grove Press.

———. 1967. *Gesammelte Werke in Acht Bänden*. Frankfurt a. M. : Suhrkamp Verlag.

———. 1973. *Arbeitsjournal 1938–1942*. Frankfurt a. M. : Suhrkamp Verlag.

———. 1980. *Prosa. Band 1–4*. Frankfurt a. M. : Suhrkamp Verlag.

———. 1981. "Against Seduction, " in Hans Küng *Art and the Question of Meaning*. New York: Crossroad.

———. 1993a. *Arbeitsjournal 1938 bis 1942*. Frankfurt a. M. : Suhrkamp Verlag.

———. 1993b. *Arbeitsjournal 1942 bis 1955*. Frankfurt a. M. : Suhrkamp Verlag.

——. 1994. *Der Untergang des Egoisten*. Johann Fatzer. Frankfurt a. M. : Suhrkamp Verlag.

——. 2002. *Die Hochzeit und andere Einakter*. Frankfurt a. M. : Suhrkamp Verlag.

——. 2003. *Kalendergeschichten*. Frankfurt a. M. : Suhrkamp Verlag.

——, 2007a. "Songs" in Th. Beckmann. *Berlin:Songs of Love and War, Peace and Exile*. München: Winter and Winter.

——. 2007b. *The Three Penny Opera*, DVD. Directed by G. W. Pabst. New York: United Film Enterprises.

Buber. Martin. 1937, I and Thou, transl. by Ronald Gregor Smith, Edinburgh T. and T. Clark, 2nd Edition New York: Scribners, 1958. 1st Scribner Classics ed. New York, NY: Scribner, 2000, c1986

——, 1952, Eclipse of God, New York: Harper and Bros. Publ. 2nd Edition Westport, Conn. : Greenwood Press, 1977.

——. 1957, Pointing the Way, transl. Maurice Friedman. New York: Harper, 1957, 2nd Edition New York: Schocken, 1974.

——, 1960, The Origin and Meaning of Hasidism, transl. M. Friedman, New York: Horizon Press.

1965, The Knowledge of Man, transl. Ronald Gregor Smith and Maurice Friedman, New York: Harper & Row. 2nd Edition New York, 1966.

1966, The way of response: Martin Buber; selections from his writings, edited by N. N. Glatzer. New York: Schocken Books.

——, 1967a, A Believing Humanism: My Testament, translation of Nachlese (Heidelberg

transl. by M. Friedman, New York: Simon and Schuster.

——, 1967b, On Judaism, edited by Nahum Glatzer and transl. by Eva Jospe and others, New York: Schocken Books.

——, 1968, On the Bible: Eighteen Studies, edited by Nahum Glatzer, New York: Schocken Books.

——, 1970a, I and Thou, a new translation with a prologue "I and you" and notes by Walter Kaufmann, New York: Scribner's Sons.

——, 1970b, Mamre: essays in religion, translated by Greta Hort. Westport, Conn. : Greenwood Press.

——, 1970c, Martin Buber and the theater, including Martin Buber's "mystery play" Elijah. Edited and translated with three introductory essays by Maurice Friedman. New York, Funk & Wagnalls.

——, 1972, Encounter; autobiographical fragments. La Salle, Ill. : Open Court.

——, 1973a, On Zion; the history of an idea. With a new foreword by Nahum N. Glatzer. Translated from the German by Stanley Godman. New York: Schocken Books.

——, 1973b, Meetings. Edited with an introd. and bibliography by Maurice Friedman. La Salle, Ill. : Open Court Pub. Co., 3rd ed. London, New York: Routledge, 2002.

——, 1983, A land of two peoples: Martin Buber on Jews and Arabs, edited with commentary by Paul R. Mendes-Flohr. New York: Oxford University Press, 2nd Edition Gloucester, Mass. : Peter Smith, 1994

——, 1985, Ecstatic confessions, edited by Paul Mendes-Flohr; translated by Esther Cameron. San Francisco: Harper & Row.

——, 1991a, Chinese tales: Zhuangzi, sayings and parables and Chinese ghost and love stories, translated by Alex Page; with an introduction by Irene Eber. Atlantic Highlands, N. J. : Humanities Press International.

——, 1991b, *Tales of the Hasidim*, foreword by Chaim Potok. New York : Schocken Books, distributed by Pantheon.

——, 1992, *On intersubjectivity and cultural creativity*, edited and with an introduction by S. N. Eisenstadt. Chicago: University of Chicago Press.

——, 1994, *Scripture and translation. Martin Buber and Franz Rosenzweig*; translated by Lawrence Rosenwald with Everett Fox. Bloomington: Indiana University Press.

——, 1999a, *The first Buber: youthful Zionist writings of Martin Buber*, edited and translated from the German by Gilya G. Schmidt. Syracuse, N. Y. : Syracuse University Press.

——, 1999b, *Martin Buber on psychology and psychotherapy: essays, letters, and dialogue*, edited by Judith Buber Agassi ; with a foreword by Paul Roazin. New York: Syracuse University Press.

——, 1999c, *Gog and Magog: a novel*, translated from the German by Ludwig Lewisohn. Syracuse, NY: Syracuse University Press.

2002a, *The legend of the Baal-Shem,* translated by Maurice Friedman. London: Routledge.

2002b, *Between man and man,* translated by Ronald Gregor-Smith; with an introduction by Maurice Friedman. London, New York: Routledge.

——, 2002c, *The way of man: according to the teaching of Hasidim,* London: Routledge.

——, 2002d, *The Martin Buber reader: essential writings,* edited by Asher D. Biemann. New York: Palgrave Macmillan.

2002e, *Ten rungs: collected Hasidic sayings,* translated by Olga Marx. London: Routledge.

——, 2003, *Two types of faith,* translated by Norman P. Goldhawk with an afterword by David Flusser. Syracuse, N. Y. : Syracuse University Press.

Bultmann, Rudolf. 1958. *Jesus Christ and Mythology,* New York: Charles Scribner's Sons.

——. 1961. *Kerygma and Myth.* New York: Harper and Row, Publishers.

Byrd. Dustin, 2011. *Ayatollah Khomeii and the Anatomy of the Islamic Revolution in Iran. Toward a Theory of Prophetic Charisma.* Lanham: University Press of America.

Cessna, Vicki. 2011. "Fisrt Bishop for the Diocese of Kalamazoo laid to rest. The Most Reverend Paul V. Donovan. September 1, 1924 -April 28. 2011. " in *The Good News. The Official Publication for the Catholoc Diocese of Kalamazoo.* Volume 14. Issue 6. June

Chardin,Pierre Teilhard De.1959.*Der Mensch im Kosmos.*München : Verlag C.h Beck

Cone,James,H.1970.Liberation. A Black Thelogy of Liberation. Philadelphia:J.B.Lippincot Company Company

Dannemann, Rüdiger. 2011. "Bob Dylan wird 70" in Neue Gesellschaft/Frankfurter Hefte 5/58.

Dragicevic, Berta/Orjar Oyen. 2009. *Fragments of Memories of Liofe and Wiork at Inter-University Centre Dubrovnik 1971-2007.* Dubrovnik, Croatia. IUC.

Dragicevic, Berta. 2011. " Interview". May 4.

Drewermann, Eugen. 1989. *Psychoanalyse und Moraltheologie. Vol1: Angst und Schuld.* Mainz: Matthias–Grünewald Verlag.

——. 1992a. *Psychoanalyse und Moraltheologie>Vol. 2:Wege und Umwege der Liebe*. Mainz: Matthias–Grünewald Verlag.

——. 1992b. *Psychoanalyse und Moraltheologie. Vol. 3:An den Grenzen des Lebens*. Mainz: Matthias–Grünewald Verlag.

——. 1992c. Worum es eigentlich geht. Protokoll einer Verurteilung. München: Kösel Verlag.

Dirks, Walter. 1968. *Die Antwort Der Mönche: Zukunftsentwürfe Aus Kritischer Zeit Von Benedikt, Franziskus, Dominikus Und Ignatius. Geschichtsauftrag Der Ordensstifter*. Olten und Freiburg im Breuisgau: Walter Verlag.

——. 1983a. *Der singende Stotterer Autobiographische Texte*. München: Kossel Verlag.

——. 1983b. *War ich ein linker Spinner? Republikanische Texte – von Weimar bis Bonn. Mit einem Vorwort von Fritz Boll*. München: Kösel Verlag.

——. 1985. *Die Samariter und der Mann aus Samaria. Vom Umgang mit der Barmherzigkeit.*
Freiburg im Breisgau: Lambertus Verlag.

——. 1987. Discourse with Walter Dirks in his home in the Black Forest. May.

——. 1988. Discourse with Walter Dirks in his home in the Black Forest. May.

Dragicevic, Berta/Orjar Oyen. 2009. Fragments of Memories of Life and Work at Inter-University Centre Dubrovnik 1971-2007

Eliade, Mircea. 1961.   *The Sacred and the Profane: The Nature of Religion*. New York: Harper and Row.

Engels, Friedrich. 1967. *The German Revolutions: The Peasant War in Germany and Germany: Revolution and Counter-Revolution*. Chicago: University of Chicago Press.

Epstine, Catherine. 2011. *Model Nazi:Arthu Greiser and the Occupation of Western Poland*. Oxford : Oxford University Press

Fergusan, Charles. 2010. "Inside Job", PG13. DVD Video. Sony Pictures Cassics. Representational

Pictures. 2011 Layout and Design Sony Pictures Home Entertainment

Feuerbach, Ludwig. 1904. *Das Wesen des Christentum*. Leipzig: Philipp eclam .

——. 1957. *The Essence of Christianity.* New York: Harper and Row Publishers.

——. 1996. *Entwürfe zu einer Neuen Philosophie.* Hamburg: Felox Meiner Verlag.

Flechtheim, Ossip K. 1959. "Sozialistischer Humanismus–eine dritte Position" in the *Frankfurter Hefte: Zeitschrift für Kultur und Politik.* 14 (9):625–634.

——. 1962. " Humanismus und Menschenrechte" in the *Frankfurter Hefte; Zeitschrift für*
Kultur und Politik. September 31/9:27-34.

——. 1963. "Die Neue Linke in der Neuen Welt" in the *Frankfurter Hefte: Zeitschrift für Kultur und Politik* 18 (XX):148–150.

——. 1966. "Widerstände gegen Abrüstung" in thr *Frankfurter Hefte, Zeitschrift für Kultur und Politik.* July 21/7:455-464.

——. 1971. *Futurologie: Der Kampf um die Zukunft.* Koln:Verlag. Wissenschaft und Politik.

Flechtheim, Ossip K. and Hans-Martin Lohmann. 2003. *Marx: Zur Einführung.* Hamburg: Junius Verlag.

Freud, Sigmund. 1939. Moses and Monotheism. New York: Random House.

——. 1946. *Totem and Taboo.* New York: Random House.

——. 1955. *Abriss der Psychoanalyse. Das Unbehagen in der Kultur.* Frankfurt a. M. /Hamburg: Fischer Bücherei.

——. 1962a. *Complete Psychoanalytical Works.* London.

——. 1962b. *Civilization and its Discontent.* New York:W. W. Norton and Company.

——. 1964. *The Future of an Illusion.* New York: Doubleday Company.

——. 1969. *Gesammelte Werke. Band X.* Frankfurt a. M. : Suhrkamp Verlag

——. 1977. *Introductory Lectures on Psychoanalysis.* New York: W. W. Norton and Company.

——. 1992. *Das Ich und das Es. Metapsychologische Schriften.* Frankfurt a. M. : Fischer Verlag.

——. 1993. *Bruchstück einer Hysterie–Analyse.* Frankfurt a. M. : Fischer Tasschenbuch.

——. 1995a. *Analyse der Phobie eines F¨nfjährigen Knaben.* Frankfurt a. M. : Fischer Verlag.

——. 1995b. *Der Wahn und die Träume in Wilhelm Jensens 'Gravida. ' Mit der Erzählung von Wilhelm Jensen*. Frankfurt a. M. : Fischer Verlag.

Fromm, Erich. 1932a. "Über Methode und Aufgabe einer analytischen Sozialpsychologie. "*Zeischrift für Sozialforschung*. 1 (1/2):28.

——. 1932b. "Die psychoanalytische Charakterologie und ihre Bedeutung für die Sozialpsychologie. " *Zeischrift für Sozialforschung*, 1 (1/2):253.

——. 1950. *Psychoanalysis and Religion*. New Haven–London.

——. 1956. *The Art of Loving*. New York: Harper & Row Publishers.

——. 1957. "Man is not a thing. " *Saturday Review*, March 16.

——. 1959. *Sigmund Freud's Mission*. New York: Harper and Brothers Publishers.

——. 1961. "Afterword, " in Georg Orwell's *1984*, New York; The New American Library.

——. 1964. *The Heart of Man: Its Genius for Good and Evil*. New York: Harper and Row, Publishers.

——. 1966a. M*an For Himself: An Inquiry into the psychology of Ethics*. New York: Fawcett World Library.

——. 1966b. *You Shall Be as Gods: A Radical Interpretation of the Old Testament and Its Tradition*. New York: Holt, Rinehart and Winston.

——. 1967. *Marx's Concept of Man*. New York: Frederick Ungar Publishing Company.

——. 1968. *The Revolution of Hope toward a Humanized Technology*. New York: Evanston and London: Harper and Row Publishers.

——. 1970a. "Guest Editorial: Thoughts on Bureaucracy. " *Management Science, Application Series, Urban Issues*, 16 (August, No. 12): B699–B705

—— 1970b. "Some Post-Marxian and Post-Freudian Thoughts on Religion and Religiousness, "in Johannes B. Metz, *New Quqestions of God*. New York: Herder and Herder. 146-156.

——. 1972a. *Escape From Freedom*. New York: The Hearst Corporation.

——. 1972b. "The Erich Fromm Theory of Aggression. " *New York Times Magazine*, February 27.

——. 1973. *The Anatomy of Human Destructiveness.* New York: Holt, Rinehart and Winston.

——. 1974. *Im Namen des Lebens.* Stuttgart : Deutsche Verlags-Anstalt

——. 1975. "Interview, " Feb. 16, in *L'Espresso* by Aleotti, L.

——. 1976. *To Have Or To Be?* New York: Harper and Row Publishers

——. 1980a. *Arbeiter und Angestellte am Vorabend des Dritten Reiches. Eine Sozialpsychologische Untersuchung.* Stuttgart: Deutsche Verlag-Anstalt.

——. 1980b. *Greatness and Limitation of Freud's Thought.* New York: Harper and Row.

——. 1981. *On Disobedience and Other Essays.* New York: The Seabury Press.

——. 1990a. *The Sane Society.* New York: Henry Holt and Company.

——. 1990b. *Beyond the Chains of Illusion: An Encounter with Freud and Marx.* New York: Continuum.

——. 1992. *The Dogma of Christ and Other Essays on Religion, Psychology, and Culture,* trans. by James Luther Adams. New York: Henry Holt and Company.

——. 1995. *The Essential Fromm: Life Between Having and Being.* New York: Continuum.

——. 1997. *Love, Sexuality and Matriarchy: About Gender.* Funk, Rainer (Ed.). New York: From International Publishing Corporation.

——. 1999. "Gibt es eine Ethik ohne Religiosität?" in *Fromm - Forum.* Tübingen. No. 3:34-36.

——. 2001. *Haben oder Sein.* München: Deutscher Verlag.

Fromm, Erich [ed.] 1966 c. *Socialist Humanism: An International Symposium.* Garden City, NY: Doubleday and Company.

Fromm, Erich, D. T. Suzuki, and, Richard De Martino. 1960. *Zen Buddhism and Psychoanalysis.* New York: Harper and Row.

Fromm, Erich and Ramon Xirau. 1979. *The Nature of Man.* New York: MacMillan Publishing Company.

Fuegi J. 1994. *Brecht and Company, Sex, Politics, and the Making of the Modern Drama.* New York: Grove Press.

Fuhr, Eckhard. 2003. "Der Souveränitäts–Exzess. "*Neue Gesellschaft – Frankfurter Hefte,* 50(6):17–19.

——. 2004a. "Gespräch mit Bischof Wolfgang Huber–Jeder Einzelne ist wichtig. " *Neue Gesellschaft – Frankfurter Hefte,* 51 (6):24–27.

——. 2004b. "Kehrt die Religion zurück. " *Neue Gesellschaft – Frankfurter Hefte,* 51 (6):20–23.

——. 2008. "Macht der Medien – wie weit ist es damit her?" in *Neue Gesellschaft- Frankfurter Hefte,* 55 (3):64-65.

——, 2011. "Dem Reinheitsgebot verpflchtet. Der neue Literaturpreis >Von Autoren für Autoren<", in *Neue Gesellschaft/ Frankfurter Hefte* 5/29.

Funk, Rainer. 1995. *The Essential Fromm: Life between Having and Being.* New York: Continuum.

——. 1999. *The Erich Fromm Reader.* Amherst, NY: Humanity Books.

——. 2000a. *Erich Fromm: His Life and Ideas. An Illustrated Biography,* New York, London: Continuum.

——. 2000b. *Erich Fromm heute. Zur Aktalituat seines Denkens.* München: Deutscher Taschenbuch Verlag.

Funk, Rainer, Helmut Johach, and Gerd Meyer. 2000. *Erich Fromm heute. Zur Aktualität seines Denkens.* München: Deutscher Taschembuch Verlag.

Greers, Donald. 1935. *The Incidence of Terror during the French Revolution.* Canbridge, Mass.

Grassi. Sergio. 2011. " Demokratieverfall in Italien, ", " in *Neue Gesellschaft/ Frankfurter Hefte* 5/58.

Gutierrez, Gustavo. 1973. *A Theology of Liberation. History, Politics and Salvation.* Maryknoll, New York: Orbis Books.

——. 1988. Von Gott sprechen in Unrecht und Leid - Job. Mainz:Grünewald Verlag

Haag, Karl–Heinz. 1981. Discourse with Professor Dr. Haag at his home in Frankfurt a. M-Höchst

——, 1982. Discourse with Professor Dr. Haag at his home in Frankfurt a. M-Høchst in

——, 1983. *Der Fortschritt in der Philosophie.* Frankfurt a. M. : Suhrkamp Verlag.

——. 2005. *Metaphysik als Forderung rationaler Weltauffassung.* Frankfurt a. M. : Humanities On Line.

Habermas, Jürgen. 1962. Strukturwandel der Öffentlichkeit. Untersuchungen zu einer Kategorie der bürgerlichen Gesellschaft. Neuwied: Hermann Luchterhand Verlag.

——, 1969. Antworten auf Herbert Marcuse. Frankfurt a. M. : Suhrkamp Verlag.

——. 1970. *Toward a Rational Society: Student Protest, Science and Politics*. Boston: Beacon Press.

——. 1971. *Knowledge and Human Interests*. Boston: Beacon Press.

——. 1973. *Zur Logik der Sozialwissenschaften*. Frankfurt a. M. : Suhrkamp Verlag.

——. 1975. *Legitimation Crisis*. Boston: Beacon Press.

——. 1976. *Zur Rekonstruktion des historischen Materialismus*. Frankfurt a. M. : Suhrkamp Verlag.

——. 1977. Discourse with Professor Habermas at Villa Nova University, USA

——. 1978a. *Theorie und Praxis*. Frankfurt a. M. : Suhrkamp Verlag.

——. 1978b. *Starnberg Studien I. Die gesellschaftliche Oriemtierung des wissenschaftlichen Fortschritts*. Frankfurt a. M: Suhrkamp Verlag.

——. 1978c. *Politik, Kunst, Religion*. Stuttgart: Reclam Verlag.

——. 1978d. Discourse with Professor Habermas in the IUC, Dubrovnik Yugoslavia.

——. 1979a. *Stichworte zur 'Geistigen Situation der Zeit' 1. Band: Nation und Republik*. Frankfurt a. M. : Suhrkamp Verlag.

——. 1979b. *Stichworte zur 'Geistigen Situation der Zeit' 2. Band: Politik und Kultur*. Frankfurt a. M. : Suhrkamp Verlag.

——. 1981a. *Kleine Politische Schriften I–IV*. Frankfurt a. M. : Suhrkamp Verlag.

——. 1981b. "Modernity versus Postmodernity. " *New German Critique* 22:3-14

——. 1982. "Tod in Jerusalem. Am Grab von Gershom Scholem—am Ende einer Ära. " *Merkur. Deutsche Zeitschrift für europäisches Denken*, Heft 4, 36.

——. 1983. *Moralbewusstsein und kommunikatives Handeln*. Frankfurt a. M. : Suhrkamp Verlag.

——. 1984a. *Vorstudien und Ergänzungen zur Theorie des kommunikativen Handelns*. Frankfurt a. M. : Suhrkamp Verlag.

——. 1984b. *The Theory of Communicative Action. Volume One: Reason and the Rationalization of Society*. Translated by Thomas McCarthy. Boston: Beacon Press.

——. 1985a. *Der philosophische Diskurs der Moderne: Zwölf Vorlesungen*. Frankfurft a. M. : Suhrkamp Verlag.

———. 1985b. *Die Neue Unübersichtlichkeit*. Frankfurt a. M. : Suhrkamp Verlag.

———. 1986. *Autonomy and Solidarity: Interviews*. London: Verso Verlag.

———. 1987a. *Eine Art Schadensabwicklung*. Frankfurt a. M. : Suhrkamp Verlag.

———. 1987b. *Philosophisch–Politische Profile*. Frankfurt a. M. : Suhrkamp Verlag.

———. 1987c. *The Philosophical Discourse of Modernity: Twelve Lectures*. Translated by Frederick G. Lawrence. Cambridge: MIT Press.

———. 1987d. *The Theory of Communicative Action. Volume Two: Lifeworld and System: A Critique of Functionalist Reason*. Translated by Thomas McCarthy. Boston: Beacon Press.

———. 1988a. *Nachmetaphysisches Denken. Philosophische Aufsätze*. Frankfurt a. M. :Suhrkamp Verlag.

———. 1988b. "Walter Benjamin: Consciousness-Raising or Rescuing Critique" in Gary Smith, [ed.] *On Walter Benjamin: Critical Essays and Recollections*. Cambridge: MIT Press.

———. 1990. *Die nachholende Revolution*. Frankfurt a. M. : Suhrkamp Verlag.

———. 1991a. *Texte und Kontexte*. Frankfurt a. M. : Suhrkamp Verlag.

———. 1991b. *Erläuterungen zur Diskursethik*. Frankfurt a. M: Suhrkamp Verlag.

———. 1991c. *Vergangenheit als Zukunft*. Zürich: Pendo Verlag.

———. 1992a. *Faktizität und Geltung. Beiträge zur Diskurstheorie des Rechts und des Demokratischen Rechtsstaates*. Frankfurt a. M. : Suhrkamp Verlag.

———. 1992b. *Post–Metaphysical Thinking: Philosophical Essays*. Cambridge: MIT Press.

———. 1992c. Discourse with Professor Habermas in the Philosophical Faculty of the Johann Wolfgang von Goethe Universität, Frankfurt a. M.

———. 1995. *Die Normalitat einer Berliner Republik*. Frankfurt a. M. : Suhrkamp Verlag.

———. 1997a. *Die Einbeziehung des Anderen. Studien zur politischen Theorie*. Frankfurt a. M. : Suhrkamp Verlag.

———. 1997b. *Vom sinnlichen Eindruck zum symbolischen Ausdruck*. Frankfurt a. M. : Suhrkamp Verlag.

———. 1998. *Die Postnationale Konstellation, Politische Essays*. Frankfurt a. M. : Suhrkamp Verlag.

——. 1999. *Wahrheit und Rechtfertigung: Philosophische Aufsätze.* Frankfurt a. M. : Suhrkamp Verlag.

——. 2001a. "Dankesrede des Friedenspreisträgers: Glauben und Wissen" Frankfurter Buchmesse. Frankfurt a. M. : Oct.

——. 2001b. *Die Zukunft der menschlichen Natur. Auf dem Weg zu einer liberalen Eugenik?* Frankfurt a. M. : Suhrkamp Verlag.

——. 2001c. *Zeit der Übergänge.* Frankfurt a. M. : Suhrkamp Verlag.

——. 2002. *Religion and Rationality: Eassays on Reason, God, and Modernity.* Cambridge, MA: The MIT Press.

——. 2003a. "Die Zeit hatte einen doppelten Boden – Der Philosoph Theodor W. Adorno in den fünfziger Jahren. Eine persönliche Notiz, " *Die Zeit*, Sept. 4. [www. zeit. de/2003/37/ Habermas_2fAdorno.]

——. 2003b. *Zeitdiagnosen: Zwölf Essays.* Frankfurt a. M. : Suhrkamp.

——. 2003c. "Dual Layered Time: Reflections on T. W. Adorno in the 1950's, " *Logos: A Journal of Modern Society and Culture.* 2 (4), [www. logosjournal. com/habermas. htm] (or) [www. logosjournal. com/issue2. 4. pdf.]

——. 2004a. *Communication and the Evolution of Society.* Boston: Beacon Press.

——. 2004b. "Religion braucht neue Übersetzer. " *Rheinischer Merkur. Deustche Wochenzeitschrift für Polik. Wirschaft. Kultur.* April.

——. 2004c. "Vorpolitische moralische Grundlagen eines freiheitlichen Staates, " presentation given on Discourse Evening in the Catholic Academy in Bavaria, Germany. 1978;

——. 2005. *Zwischen Naturalismus und Religion. Philosophische Aufsatze.* Frankfurt a. M. : Suhrkamp Verlag.

——. 2006a. *Between Naturalism and Religion,* Cambridge, MA: Polity Press.

——. 2006b. "Religion in the Public Sphere. " *European Journal of Philosophy,* 14 (1):1–25.

——. 2006c. *The Divided West. Cambridge.* Cambridge, MA: Polity Press.

——. 2006d. "Das Sprachspiel verantwortlicher Urheberschaft und das Problem der Willensfreiheit: Wie lässt sich der epistemische Dualismus mit einem ontologischen Monismus versöhnen?" *Deutsche Zeitschrift für Philosophie.* 54 (5).

——. 2007. "Ein Bewusstsein von dem was fehlt. Über Glauben und Wissen und den Defaitismus der modernen Vernunft. " *Neue Zürcher Zeitung*, Feb. 10.

——. 2009. *Europe: The Faltering Project* . Malden, MA: Polity Press

Habermas, Jürgen and Sylvia Bovenschen. 1981. *Gespräch mit Herbert Marcuse*. Frankfurt a. M. : Suhrkamp Verlag.

Habermas, Jürgen and Dieter Henrich. 1974. *Zwei Reden. Aus Anlass des Hegel–Preises*. Frankfurt a. M. : Suhrkamp Verlag.

Habermas, Jürgen and Niklas Luhmann. 1975. *Theorie der Gesellschaft oder Sozialtechnologie*. Frankfurt a. M. : Suhrkamp Verlag.

Habermas, Jürgen and Joseph Ratzinger. 2006. *The Dialectics of Secularization: On Reason and Religion*, ed. by Florian Schuller, trans. by Brian McNeil. San Francisco: Ignatius Press.

Hegel. Georg W. 1896. *Lectures on the History of Philosophy*. London.

——. 1964. *Wissenschaft der Logik*. Stuttgart–Bad Cannstatt: Friedrich Frommann Verlag.

——. 1965. *Vorlesungen über die Philosophie der Religion*. Stuttgart–Bad Cannstatt: Friedrich Frommann Verlag.

——. 1969. *Vorlesungen über die Philosophie der Religion*. Frankfurt a. M. : Suhrkamp Verlag.

——. 1972. *Jenaer Schriften*. Berlin: Akademie Verlag.

——. 1976. *Grundlinien der Philosophie des Rechts*. Frankfurft a. M. : Suhrkamp Verlag.

——. 1979. *System of Ethical Life (1802 and 3) and First Philosophy of Spirit (Part II of the System of Speculative Philosophy 1803 and 4)*. Albany: State University of New York Press.

——. 1986a. *Frühe Schriften*. Frankfurt a. M. : Suhrkamp Verlag.

——. 1986b. *Jenaer Schriften 1801–1807*. Frankfurt a. M. : Suhrkamp Verlag.

——. 1986c. *Phänomenologie des Geistes*. Frankfurt a. M. : Suhrkamp Verlag.

——. 1986d. *Nürnberger und Heidelberger Schriften 1808–1817*. Frankfurt a. M. : Suhrkamp Verlag.

——. 1986e. *Wissenschaft der Logik I*. Frankfurt a. M. : Suhrkamp Verlag.

——. 1986f. *Wissenschaft der Logik II*. Frankfurt a. M. : Suhrkamp Verlag.

———. 1986g. *Grundlinien der Philosophie des Rechts oder Naturrecht und Staatswissenschaft im Grundriss.* Frankfurt a. M. : Suhrkamp Verlag.

———. 1986h. *Enzyklopädie der philosophischen Wissenschaften I.* Frankfurt a. M. : Suhrkamp Verlag.

———. 1986i. *Enzyklopädie der philosophischen Wissenschaften II.* Frankfurt a. M. : Suhrkamp Verlag.

———. 1986j. *Enzyklopädie der philosophischen Wissenschaften III.* Frankfurt a. M. : Suhrkamp Verlag.

———. 1986k. *Berliner Schriften 1818–1831.* Frankfurt a. M. : Suhrkamp Verlag.

———. 1986l. *Vorlesungen über die Philosophie der Geschichte.* Frankfurt a. M. : Suhrkamp Verlag.

———. 1986m. *Vorlesungen über die Ästhetik I.* Frankfurt a. M. : Suhrkamp Verlag.

———. 1986n. *Vorlesungen über die Ästhetik II.* Frankfurt a. M. : Suhrkamp Verlag.

———. 1986o. *Vorlesungen über die Ästhetik III.* Frankfurt a. M. : Suhrkamp Verlag.

———. 1986p. *Vorlesungen uber die Philosophie der Religion I.* Frankfurt a. M. : Suhrkamp Verlag.

———. 1986q. *Vorlesungen uber die Philosophie der Religion II.* Frankfurt a. M. : Suhrkamp Verlag.

———. 1986r. *Vorlesungen über die Geschicte der Philosophie I.* Frankfurt a. M. : Suhrkamp Verlag.

———. 1986s. *Vorlesungen über die Geschichte der Philosophie II.* Frankfurt a. M. : Suhrkamp Verlag.

———. 1986t. *Vorlesungen über die Geschichte der Philosophie III.* Frankfurt a. M. : Suhrkamp Verlag.

Heidegger, Martin. 1956. *Der Feldweg.* Frankfurt a. M. : Suhrkamp Verlag

———. 1968. *Existence and Being.* Chicago: Henry Regnery Company.

———. 2001. *Sein und Zeit.* Tübingen: Max Niemeyer Verlag.

Hitler, Adolf. 1943. *Mein Kampf.* Boston: Houghton Mifflin Company.

———. 1986. *Hitler's Secret Book,* introduced. by Telford Taylor, Translated by Salvator Attanasio. New York: Grove Press.

Hochgeschwender.Michael.2010.*Der amerikanische Bürgerkrieg.* München:C.H.Beck

Honneth, Axel. 1985. *Kritik der Macht. Reflexionsstufen einer kritischen Gesellschaftstheorie.* Frankfurt a. M. : Suhrkamp Verlag.

———. 1990. *Die zerissene Welt des Sozialen. Sozialphilosophische Aufsätze.* Frankfurt a. M. : Suhrkamp Verlag.

———. 1993. *Kommunitarismus – Eine Debatte über die moralischen Grundlagen moderner Gesellschaften.* Frankfurt a. M. : Campus Verlag.

———. 1994. *Kampf um Anerkennung: Zur moralischen Grammatik sozialer Konflikte.* Frankfurt a. M. : Suhrkamp Verlag.

———. 1996a. *The Struggle for Recognition: The Moral Grammar of Social Conflicts.* Cambridge, MA: The MIT Press.

———. 1996b. "Die soziale Dynamik von Mißachtung Zur Ortsbestimmung einer kritischen Gesellschaftstheorie. " *Mitteilungen des Instituts für Sozialforschung,* 7 (Jun.):13–32.

———. 2000. *Das Andere der Gerechtigkeit: Aufsätze zur praktischen Philosophie.* Frankfurt a. M. : Suhrkamp Verlag.

———. 2001. "Zur Zukunft des Instituts für Sozialfroschung. " *Mitteilungen des Instituts für Sozialforschung,* 12 (Sept.):54–63.

———. 2002a. *Befreiung aus der Mündigkeit: Paradoxien des gegenwärtigen Kapitalismus.* Frankfurt a. M. : Campus Verlag.

———. 2002b. "Vorbemerkung. " *Mitteilungen des Instituts für Sozialforschung,* 13 (Sept. : 47–50.

———. 2004. "Anerkennung als Ideology, " *West End I,* Jahrgang, Heft 1, Frankfurt.

———. 2005. *Verdinglichung: Eine anerkennungstheoretische Studie.* Frankfurt a. M: Suhrkamp Verlag.

———. 2007. *Pathologien der Vernunft: Geschichte und Gegenwart der Kritischen Theorie,* Frankfurt a. M: Suhrkamp Verlag.

Honneth, Axel and Hans Joas. 2002. *Kommunikatives Handeln: Beiträge zu Jürgen Habermas'Theorie des kommunikativen Handelns.* Frankfurt a. M. : Suhrkamp Verlag.

Hörisch, Felix. 2011. "Mehr Demokratie wagen-auch in der Wirtschaft, . " in *Neue Gesellschaft/ Frankfurter Hefte* 5/58

Horkheimer, Max. 1932. "Geschichte und Psychologie. " *Zeitschrift für Sozialforschung,* 1 (1/2):125–144.

———. 1936. "Zu Theodor Haecker: Der Christ und die Geschichte. " *Zeischrift für Sozialforschung* 5.

——. 1966. "Letzte Spur von Theologie–Paul Tillich's Vermächtnis. " *Frankfurter Allgemeine* Zeitung.

——. 1967a. *Werk und Wirken Paul Tillich's Ein Gedenkbuch.* Stuttgart: Evangelisches Verlag.

——. 1967b. *Zur Kritik der instrumentellen Vernunft. Aus den Vorträgen und Aufzeichnungen seit Kriegsende.* Frankfurt a. M. : S. Fischer Verlag.

——. 1970a. "Bemerkungen über Wissenschaft und Krise. " *Zeitschrift für Sozialforschung,* München: Kösel-Verlag.

——. 1970b. "Geschichte und Psychologie. " *Mitteilungen des Instituts für Sozialforschung.*

——. 1970c. *Kritische Theorie: Eine Dokumentation.* Frankfurt a. M. : Fischer Bücherei.

——. 1971. *Die Sehnsucht nach dem ganz Anderen. Ein Interview mit Kommentar von Helmut Gumnior.* Hamburg, Furche Verlag.

——. 1972. *The Critical Theory: Selected Essays.* New York: The Seabury Press.

——. 1973. "Foreword" in Martin Jay, *The Dialectical Imagination: A History of the Frankfurt School and the Institute for Social Research 1923–1950.* Boston and Toronto: Little Brown and Company.

——. 1974a. *Critique of Instrumental Reason.* New York: The Seabury Press.

——. 1974b. *Eclipse of Reason.* New York: The Seabury Press. ——. 1974c. *Notizen 1950 bis 1969 und Dämmerung. Notizen in Deutschland.* Frankfurt a. M. : S. Fischer Verlag.

——. 1978. *Dawn and Decline. Notes 1926–1931 and 1950–1969.* New York: The Seabury Press.

——. 1981a. *Gesellschaft im Übergang. Aufsätze. Reden und Vortrage 1942–1970.* Frankfurt a. M. : Fischer Verlag.

——. 1981b. *Sozial–philosophische Studien: Aufsätze, Reden und Vorträge 1930–1972.* Frankfurt a. M: Fischer Verlag.

——. 1981c. *Tradionelle und kritische Theorie: Vier Aufsätze.* Frankfurt a. M. : Fischer Verlag.

——. 1985g. *Vorträge und Aufzeichnungen 1949–1973.* Frankfurt a. M. : Fischer Taschenbuch Verlag.

——. 1985l. *Nachgelassene Schriften 1931–1949.* Frankfurt a. M. : Fischer Verlag.

——. 1987b. *Philosophische Frühschriften 1922–1932.* Frankfurt a. M. : Fischer Taschenbich Verlag.

——. 1987e. *Dialektik der Aufklärung' und Schriften 1940–1950.* Frankfurt a. M. : Fischer Verlag.

——. 1987i. *Nachgelassene Schriften 1914–1931.* Frankfurt a. M. : Fischer Taschenbuch Verlag.

——. 1987k. *Nachgelassene Schriften 1914–1931.* Frankfurt a. M. : Fischer Taschenbuch Verlag.

——. 1988a. *Aus der Pubertät: Novellen und Tagebuchblätter 1914–1918.* Frankfurt a. M. : Fischer Verlag.

——. 1988c. *Schriften 1931–1936.* Frankfurt a. M. : Fischer Taschenbuch Verlag.

——. 1988d. *Schriften 1936–1941.* Frankfurt a. M. : Fischer Taschenbuch Verlag.

——. 1988n. *Nachgelsassene Schriften 1949–1972.* Frankfurt a. M. : Fischer Verlag.

——. 1989m. *Nachgelassene Schriften 1949 – 1972.* Frankfurt a. M. : Suhrkamp Verlag.

——. 1990j. *Nachgelassene Schriften 1914–1931.* Frankfurt a. M. : Fischer Verlag. ——. 1991f. *'Zur Kritik der instrumentellen Vernunft' und 'Notizen 1949–1969. '* Alfred Schmidt [ed.] Frankfurt a. M. : Fischer Verlag.

——. 1995o. *Briefwechsel 1913–1936.* Frankfurt a. M. : Fischer Verlag.

——. 1995p. *Briefwechsel 1937–1940.* Frankfurt a. M. : Fischer Verlag.

——. 1996r. *Briefwechsel 1949–1973.* Frankfurt a. M: Fischer Verlag.

——. 1996q. *Briefwechsel 1941–1948.* Frankfurt a. M. : Fischer Verlag.

——. 1996s. *Nachträge, Verzeichnisse und Register.* Frankfurt a. M. : Fischer Taschenbuch Verlag.

——. 2006. "Psalm 91. " Translated by Michael R. Ott in Warren S. Goldstein, [ed.] *Marx, Critical Theory, and Religion: A Critique of Rational Choice.* Leiden: Brill Academic Publishers.

Horkheimer, Max. [Hg.] 1970. *Zeitschrif für Sozialforschung,* München: Kösel Verlag.

Horkheimer, Max and Theodor W. Adorno. 1951. "Vorurteil und Charakter. " *Frankfurter Hefte: Zeitschrift für Kultur und Politik,* 7 (4):284–291.

——. 1956. *Universität und Gesellschaft. Eine Erhebung des Instituts für Sozialforschung unter Mitwirkung des Instituts für vergleichende Sozialwissenschaften.* Frankfurt a. Main.

——. 1969a. *Dialectic of Enlightenment.* New York: The Seabury Press.

——. 1969b. *Dialektik der Aufklärung. Philosophische Fragmente.* Frankfurt a. M. : S. Fischer Verlag.

——. 1972a. *Dialectic of Enlightenment.* Translated by John Cumming. New York: The Seabury Press.

——. 1972b. *Critical Theory/Selected Essays.* New York: The Seabury Press

——. 1984. *Sociologica. Reden und Vorträge.* Frankfurt a. M: Europäische Verlag.

——. 2002. *Dialectic of Enlightenment: Philosophical Fragments*, ed. by Gunzelin Schmid Noerr [ed.] Translated by Edmund Jehcott. Stanford, California: Stanford University Press.

Horkheimer, Max, Fromm, Erich, and Marcuse, Herbert. 1936. *Studien über Autorität und Familie.* Schriften des Instituts für Sozialforschung. Paris.

Huntington, Samuel P. 1996. *The Clash of Civilizations? The Debate.* New York: Foreign Affairs, W. W. Norton.

——. 1998. *The Clash of Civilizations and the Remaking of World Order.* New York: Simon & Schuster.

Jacob, Janet. 2011. " 2010 Pao; Hanley Furfey Lectures. Sacred Space and Collective Memory: Memoralizing Genocide at Sites of Terror. " In *Sociology of Religion. A Quarterly Review.* Volume 72. No. 2. Summer 2011.

Jung, Carl, G. 1933. *Modern Man in Search of a Soul.* New York: Harcourt, Brace, Jovanovich.

——. 1958. *Psyche & Symbol.* Garden City, NY: Doubleday & Company.

——. 1990. *Archetypen.* München: Deutscher Taschenbuch Verlag.

Kant, Immanuel. 1929. *Critique of Pure Reason.* New York: St. Martin's Press.

——. 1946. *Zum Ewigen Frieden.* Düsseldorf: Drei Eulen Verlag.

——. 1968. *Schriften zur Anthropologie, Geschichtsphilosophie, Politik und Pädagogik.* Frankfurt a. M. : Suhrkamp Verlag.

——. 1970. *On the Foundation of Morality: A Modern Version of the Grundlegungen.*

Bloomington, IN: Indiana University Press.

———. 1974a. *Die Religion innerhalb der Grenzen der blossen Vernunft.* Stuttgart: Philipp Reclam.

———. 1974b. *Kritik der Urteilskraft.* Frankfurt a. M; Suhrkamp Verlag.

———. 1975. *Was ist Aufklärung? Aufsätze zur Geschichte und Philosophie.* Göttingen: Vandenhoeck and Ruprecht.

———. 1981. *Zum ewigen Frieden.* Stuttgart: Philipp Reclam Jun.

———. 1982. *Kritik der praktischen Vernunft. Grundlegung zur Metaphysik der Sitten.* Frankfurt a. M. : Suhrkamp Verlag.

———. 1983. *Anthropologie in Pragmatischer Hinsicht.* Stuttgart: Philipp Reclam Verlag.

Karpov, Vyacheslav. 2010. "Desecularization: A Conceptual Framework, " in Journal of Church and State. Vol. 52, no 2, 232 -270

Keegan.John.2010.*Der amerikanische Bürgerkrieg.*Berlion :Rowohlt

Kesting,Hanjo.2011."Der grosse Mythos und die kleine LadyHarriet Beacher Stowe." In *Die Neue esellschaft.Frankfurter Hefte* 6/58: 68-70.

KoenigsbergerRichard A. 2011. *Hitler, the Holocaust and War: the Final Solution.* Elmhurst New Yoek:Library of Social Science

Kogon, Eugen. 1965. *Der SS–Staat. Das System der Deutschen Konzentrationslager.* Frankfurt a. M. : Europäische Verlag.

———. 1967. "Revolution und Theologie–Das Neue in unserem Zeitalter. Ein Symposion. *"Frankfurter Hefte,* Sept. 22 (9).

———. 1995. *Der SS–Staat. Das System der Deutschen Konzentrationslager.* München: Wilhelm Heyne Verlag.

———. 2002. *Der SS Staat.* Frankfurt a. M. : Europäische Verlag.

Kogon, Michael. 2003a. "Bilanz des Eugen–Kogon–Jahres 2003. " *Neue Gesellschaft – Frankfurter Hefte,* 50 (3).

———. 2003b. "Kurze Geschichte der Erinnerung an meinen Vater. " *Neue Gesellschaft – Frankfurter Hefte,* 50 (3):59–63.

Kolodiejchuk,Brian.2007.Mother Teresa.Come Be My Light,The Private Writings of the " Saint of Calcutta.New York : Doubleday

Krell, Christian. 2011. " Was man aus den socialdemoratischen Reformdiskursen lernen kann., "*Neue Gesellschaft/ Frankfurter Hefte* 5/58

Krell, Christian/Tobias Mörschel 2011. "Demokratie in Deutschland 2011. " in *Neue Gesellschaft/ Frankfurter Hefte* 5/ 58.

Küng, Hans. 1970. *Menschwerdung Gottes: Eine Einführung in Hegel's Theologisches Denken als Prolegomena zu einer künftigen Christologie.* Freiburg: Herder Verlag.

——. 1972. *Freiheit des Christen.* Hamburg: Siebenstern Taschenbuch Verlag.

——. 1976. *The Church.* Garden City, NY: Double Day and Co.

——. 1978. *Existiert Gott? Antwort auf die Gottesfrage der Neuzeit.* München: R. Piper Verlag.

——. 1980. *Wegzeichen in die Zukunft. Programmatisches für eine christlichere Kirche.* Reinbeck bei Hamburg: Rowohlt Taschenbuch Verlag.

——. 1981a. *Art and the Question of Meaning.* New York: Crossroad.

——. 1982. *Ewiges Leben?* München: R. Piper Verlag.

——. 1989. *Unfehlbar? Eine unerledigte Anfrage. Mit einem aktuellen Vorwort von Herbert Haag.* Munchen: Piper Verlag.

——. 1990a. *Freud and the Problem of God.* New Haven: Yale University Press.

——. 1990b. *Projekt Weltethos.* Munchen: Piper Verlag

——. 1991a. *World Religions: Universal Peace. Global Ethic.* Tübingen: Foundation Global Ethic. [www. weltethos. org/pdf_dat/ ausstellung_eng. pdf

——. 1991b. *Das Judentum.* München: Piper Verlag.

——. 1992. *Theologie im Aufbruch: Eine ökumenische Grundlegung.* München: Piper Verlag.

——. 1993a. *24 Thesen zur Gottesfrage.* Munchen: Piper Verlag.

——. 1993b. *Credo. Das Apostolische Glaubensbekenntnis–Zeitgenossen erklärt.* München: Piper Verlag.

——. 1994a. *Das Christentum. Wesen und Geschichte* München : Piper Verlag.

——. 1994b. *Grosse Christliche Denker,* München: Piper Verlag.

——. 1998. *Mozart–Spuren der Transzendenz.* Munchen: Piper Verlag.

——. 2004. *Der Islam. Geschichte, Gegenwart, Zukunft:* München: Piper Verlag.

——. 2009. "Wenn der Papst ein Obama wäre, "in *Süddeutsche Zeitung,* January 31.

Küng, Hans, Joseph van Ess, Heinrich von Stietencron, and Heinz Bechert. 1984. *Christentum, und Weltreligionen: Islam, Hinduismus, Buddhismus.* München: Piper Verlag.

Küng, Hans and Rabbi Walter Homolka. 2009. *How to Do Good and Avoid Evil: A Global Ethic from the Sources of Judaism.* Woodstock, Vermont: Skylight Path Publishing.

Küng, Hans and Karl-Josef Kuschel. 1993a. *A Global Ethic. The Declaration of the Parliament of the World's Religions.* New York:Continuum.

———. 1993b. *Weltfrieden durch Religionsfrieden. Antworten aus den Weltreligionen.* München: Piper Verlag.

Kuschel, Karl–Josef. 1990. *Welches Christentum hat Zukunft. Dorothee Sölle und Johann Baptist Metz.* Stuttgart: Kreuz Verlag.

Kuschel, Karl-Josef and Stephan Schlensog. 2008. *Hans Küng-eine Nahaufnahme.* München: Piper Verlag.

Lefebvre, Henri. 1982. *The Sociology of Marx.* New York : Comlubia University Press

Leibniz, G. W. 1996. *Die Theodizee von der Güte Gottes, der Freiheit des Menschen und den Ursprug des Ubels, I. Philosophische Schriften 2 and 1.* Frankfurt a. M. : Suhrkamp Verlag.

Lenin, V. I., 1972. *Collected Works.* Moscow .

Lieber, David L. 2001. *Etz Hayim: Torah and Commentary.* New York: The Rabbinical Assembly.

Lohmann,Hans-Martin.2011."Korrektur eines Mythos?Neues über Echnaton."in *Neue Gesellschaft/Frankfurter* Hefte. 6/58.

Longerich Peter. 2011a. *Holocaust:The Nazi Persecution and Murder of the Jews.* Oxford: Oxford University Press

———2011b:*Heinrich Himmler: Biographie.* Berlin: Siedler Verlag

Lortz, Joseph. 1962a. *Die Reformation in Deutschland. Band I. Vorraussetzungen. Aufbruch. Erste Entscheidungen.* Freiburg: Herder.

———. 1962b. *Die Reformation in Deutschland. Band II. Ausbau der Fronten. Unionsversuche. Ergebnis.* Freiburg: Herder.

———. 1964. *Geschichte der Kirche.* Munster: Verlag. Aschendorff.

Lucke von,Albrecht.2011."Symptom der ModerneDer Messie oder der Chaosmensch," in *Neue Gesellschaft/Frankfurter Hefte*6/ 58: 62-64

Lundgren, Svante. 1998. *Fight Against Idols. Erich Fromm on Religion, Judaism and the Bible.* Frankfurt a. M. : Pter Lang

Maas, Heika. 2011. " Fortschritt und Demoratisierung, " in *Neue Gesellschaft/ Frankfurter Hefte* 5/58

Maciejewski,Franz.2010.*Echnaton oder Die Erfindung des Monotheismus. Zur Korrektur eines Mythos*. Berlin : Osburg Verlag .

Marcuse, Herbert. 1960. *Reason and Revolution: Hegel and the Rise of Social Theory*. Boston: Beacon Press.

——. 1961. *Soviet Marxism: A Critical Analysis*. New York: Random House.

——. 1962. *Eros and Civilization: A Philosophical Inquiry into Freud*. New York: Vintage Books.

——. 1965. "The Ideology of Death" in H. Feifel (Ed), *The Meaning of Death*. New York

——. 1967. *One Dimensional Man: Studies in the Ideology of Advanced Industrial Society*. Boston: Beacon Press.

——. 1969a. *Negations: Essays in Critical Theory*. Boston: Beacon Press.

——. 1969b. *An Essay on Liberation*. Boston: Beacon Press.

——. 1970a. "Marxism and the New Humanity: An Unfinished Revolution. " Chapter 1, in J. Raines and Th. Dean [ed.], *Marxism and Radical Religion*. Philadelphia: Temple University.

——. 1970b. *Five Lectures*. Boston: Free Press.

——. 1973. *Studies in Crirtical Philosophy*. Boston: Beacon Press.

——. 1975. *Zeit-Messungen*. Frankfurt a. M: Suhrkamp Verlag.

——. 1979. *Kultur und Gesellschaft 2*. Frankfurt a. M. : Suhrkamp Verlag

——. 1980a. *Psychoanalyse und Politik*. Frankfurt a. M. : Europäische Verlag.

——. 1980b. *Kultur und Gesellschaft 1*. Frankfurt a. M. : Suhrkamp Verlag.

——. 1984. *Aufsätze und Vorlesungen 1948–1969*. Versuch über die Befreiung. Frankfurt a. M. : Suhrkamp Verlag.

——. 1987. *Hegel's Ontology and the Theory of Historicity*. Cambridge, MA: The MIT Press.

——. 1995. *Triebstruktur und Gesellschaft*. Frankfurt a. M. : Suhrkamp Verlag.

——. 2001. *Toward a Critical Theory of Society*. London and New York: Routledge.

——. 2005. *Heideggerian Marxism*. Lincon: University of Nebraska Press.

Marr, Andrew. 2011. " Letter to R. J. Siebert"from May 25.

Marx, Karl. 1871. *Zweiter Entwurf zum 'Bürgerkrieg in Frankreich'*. New York: The Modern Library.

——. 1906. *Capital: A Critique of Political Economy*. New York: The Modern Library.

——. 1951. *Zur Kritik der politischen Ökonomie*. Berlin: Dietz Verlag.

——. 1953. *Die Frühschriften*. Stuttgart: Alfred Kröner Verlag.

——. 1956. *Karl Marx: Selected Writings in Sociology and Social Philosophy*. Translated by T. B. Bottomore, Foreward by Erich Fromm. New York: MacGraw Hill.

——. 1961a. *Das Kapital. Kritik der politischen Ökonomnie Buch I. Erster Band: Der Productionsprozess des Kapitals*, Berlin: Dietz Verlag.

——. 1961b. *Das Kapital. Kritik der politischen Ökonomnie Buch II: Der Zirkulationsprozeß des Kapital*. Berlin: Dietz Verlag.

——. 1961c. *Das Kapital: Kritik der politischen Ökonomie. Buch III, Dritter Band: Der Gesamtprozess der kapitalistischen Produktion*. Berlin: Dietz Verlag.

——. 1963. *The 18th Brumaire of Louis Bonaparte*. New York: International Publishers.

——. 1964. *Early Writings*. Translated by T. B. Bottomore. New York: McGraw–Hill Book Company.

——. 1974. "A Contribution to the Critique of Hegel's Philosophy of Right. Introduction" in Karl Marx, *Early Writings*. London: Penguin Books.

——. 1977. *Capital*. Volume 1. New York: Vintage Books.

——. 2000. "Economic and Philosophic Maniscripts of 1844" transcribed by Andy Blunden in marxists. org

Marx, Karl and Friedrich Engels. 1953a. *Ausgewählte Schriften, Band I*. Berlin: Dietz Verlag .

——. 1953b. *Ausgewählte Schriften, Band II*. Berlin: Dietz Verlag.

——. 1953c. *Die Heilige Familie und andere Philosophische Frühschriften*. Berlin: Dietz Verlag.

——. 1955. *The Communist Manifesto. New* York: Appleton-Century Crofts.

——. 1960. *Die deutsche Ideologie, Kritik der neuesten deutschen Philosophie in ihren* Repräsentanten Feuerbach, B. Bauer und

Stirner, und des deutschen Sozialismus in *seinen verschiedenen Propheten*. Berlin: Dietz Verlag.

——. 2005. *The Communist Manifesto and Other Writings*. New York: Barnes and Noble Classics.

McPherson.James M.. 2010.*Battle Cry of Freedom*.New York : Penguin

Meier. Horst. 2011. "Spassgrundrecht auf Selbstbestimmung. Unsere neue Datenwelt und die 'informationelle Selbstbestimmung'" in *Neue Geselschaft /. Frankfurter Hefte* 5/ 58.

Mercieca, Charles. 2011a. "Self-Proclaimed Pro-Life American Politicans in True Perspective, "in mercieca@knology. net. May 23.

——. 2011b, " Global Harmony: realization of World peace, " in mercieca@knology. net. May June 14. .

——. 2011c. "The Arrogance of Authority, " in mercieca@knology. net. May June 18.

——. 2011d. "Divine Versus Human Mind, " in mercieca@knology. net July 8.

——. 2011e. "Awesome Photo- See for Yourself: God Parting the Sky. " In<mercieca@knology, net>Metz, Johannes B. 1959. *Advent Gottes*. München: Verlag. Ars Sacra.

——. 1962. *Cristliche Anthropozentrik*. München: Kösel Verlag.

——. 1963. *Hörer des Wortes: Zur Grundlegung einer Religionsphilosophie*. München: Kösel Verlag.

——. 1965. *The Church in the World*. New York: Paulist Press.

——. 1967. *The Evolving World and Theology*. New York: Paulist Press.

——. 1969. *Reform und Gegen–Reformation Heute, Zwei Thesen zur ökumenischen Situation der kirche*. Mainz: Matthias Grünewald Verlag.

——. 1970. *Befreiendes Gedächtnis Jesu Christi*. Mainz: Matthias Grünewald Verlag.

——. 1972a. "Erinnerung des Leidens als Kritik eines teleogisch–technologischen Zukunftsbegriffes. " *Evangelische Theologie*.

——. 1972b. "Zukunft aus dem Gedächtnis des Leidens. " *Concilium*.

——. 1973a. "Erinnerung. " *Handbuch philosophischer Grundbegriffe*. I., Munchen.

——. 1973b. "Erlösung und Emanzipation" in L. Scheffczyk [ed.], *Erlösung und Emanzipation,* Freiburg.

——. 1973c. *Theology of the World.* New York: The Seabury Press.

——. 1975a. "Karl Rahner–ein theologisches Leben" in *Stimmen der Zeit.*

——. 1975b. "Unsere Hoffnung. Ein Bekenntnius des Glaubens in dieser Zeit. Vorlage zur Gemeinsame Synode der Bistumer in der Bundesrepubliik Deutschland, " in *Synode 6.*

——. 1977. *Glaube in Geschichte und Gesellschaft. Studien zu einer praktischen Fundamentaltheologie,* Mainz: Matthias–Grunewald–Verlag.

——. 1978. *Zeit der Orden? Zur Mystik und Politik der Nachfolge.* Freiburg: Herder Verlag.

——. 1980. *Jenseits bürgerlicher Religion. Reden uber die Zukunft des Christentusm,* Munchen: Chr. Kaiser Verlag.

——. 1981. *The Emergent Church.* New York: Cross Road.

——. 1984. *Den Glauben lernen und lehren. Dank an Karl Rahner.* München: Kösel Verlag.

——. 1995. *Landschaft aus Schreien. Zur Dramatik der Theodizee Frage.* Mainz: Matthias Grünewald Verlag.

——. 1997. *Zum Begriff der neuen Politischen Theologie 1967–1997.* Mainz: Matthias–Grunewald–Verlag.

——. 1998. *A Passion for God. The Mystical-Political Dimension of Christianity.* New York: Paulist Press.

Metz, Johann B., Jürgen Habermas, and Dorothy Sölle, et al. 1994. *Diagnosen zur Zeit.* Düsseldorf: Patmos Verlag.

Metz, Johann B. and Tiemo R. Peters. 1991. *Gottespassion: Zur Ordensexistenz heute.* Freiburg: Herder Verlag.

Metz, Johann B. and T Rendtorf [eds.] 1971. *Die Theologie in der interdisziplinären Forschung.* Bertelsmann: Universitäts Verlag.

Metz, Johannes B. and Elie Wiesel. 1993. *Trotzdem hoffen.* Mainz: Matthias Grünewald Verlag.

Moltmann, Jürgen. 1969. *Theologie der Hoffnung. Untersuchungen zur Begründung und zu den Konsequenzen einer christlichen Eschatologie.* München: Chr. Kaiser Verlag.

——. 1996. *The Coming of God: Christian Eschatology.* Minneapolis: Fortress Press.

——. 2002a. "Die Endzeit hat begonnen. Warum viele Amerikaner die Bibel als verschlüsselten Fahrplan der Weltgeschichte

lesen, " *Die Zeit,* [www. zeit. de/2002/51/Weltuntergang.]
——. 2002b. *Wissenschaft und Weisheit: Zumj Gesprach zwischen naturwissenschaft undTheologie.* Gutersloh: Gutersloher Verlag.

Moore, Michael. 2009. Capitalism : A ove Story. "Overture Films. LLC. Paeamount . DVD. Vantage. Anchor Bay

More, Thomas. 1895. *Utopia.* Berlin: Weidmannsche Buchhandlung.

——. 1901. *Utopia.* Salt Lake City, UT: Project Gutenberg – Literary Archive Foundation. [www. gutenberg. org/etext/2130.]

——. 1963. *Utopia.* New York: Pocket Books.

Mühlleitner, Elke, 2000. " Otto Fenichel und Erich Fromm. Annäherungen in Europa. Konfikte in Amerika, "in the *Institut für Sozialforschung. An der Johann Wolfgang Goethe- Universität.* Frankfurt am Main. Mitteiungen. Heft 11. September

Neimann, Susan/" An welcher Zukunft wollen wir arbeiten? "in *Neue Gesellschaft/ Frankfurter Hefte* 5/58

Neumann, F. 1942. *Behemoth: The Structure and Practice of National Socialism,* Toronto: Oxford University Press.

Nicholas de Cusa. 1962. *Unity and Reform.* Chicago: University of Notre Dame Press.

Nida-Rümelin, Julian. 2011. " John Rawls' Theorie der Gerechtigkeit- nach 40 Jahre", " in *Neue Gesellschaft/ Frankfurter Hefte* 5/58.

Niebuhr, Reinhold. 1932. *Moral Man and Immoral Society. A Study in Ethics and Politics.* New York: Charles Scribner's Sons.

——. 1964. *Marx and Engels on Religion.* New York: Schocken Books.

Nonhoff, Martin. 2011. " Politik in der Mediendemokratie, "in *Neue Gesellschaft/ Frankfurter Hefte* 5/58.

Oelmüller, Willi [ed.] 1990. *Theodizee–Gott vor Gericht?* München: Wilhelm Fink Verlag.

——. 1992. *Worüber man nicht schweigen kann. Neue Diskussionen zur Theodizeefrage.* München: Wilhelm Fink Verlag.

Ott, Michael R. 2001. *Max Horkheimer's Critical Theory of Religion: The Meaning of Religion in the Struggle for Human Emancipation.* Lanham, MD: University Press of America.

——. 2004a. "A Critique of the Ambiguity of Bourgeois Religion: Max Horkheimer's Critical Theory of Religion" in George N. Lundskow's [ed.] *Religious Innovation in a Global Age: Essays on the Construction of Spirituality*. Jefferson, North Carolina: McFarland & Company, Inc.

——. 2004b. "L'ambiguïté sociale de la religion" in *X-Alta:Terreur et Sacralité. Dans la religion du Capital*, Henri Vaugrand [ed.] November, 8:45-62. Abjat/Bandiat, France.

——. 2004c. "A Critical Theory of Religion Critique of the Globalization of Civil Society" in *Materials of the IV International Seminar 9-11 November, 2004, in Yalta*, Tatyana A. Senyushkina [ed.] Simferopol: Tauria.

——. 2004d. From an interview with Professor Michael R. Ott, an expert in globalization, on September 16 and 17. Grand Valley State University, Allendale, Michigan. [Unpublished.]

——. 2005. "Reclaiming the Revolutionary Substance and Potential of Religion: The Critical Theory of Religion" in *Michigan Sociological Review*, 19:155-180. Joseph M. Verschave [ed.] Ann Arbor, Michigan: Huron Valley Printing.

——. 2006. "The Notion of the Totally "Other" and its Consequence in the Critical Theory of Religion and the Rational Choice Theory of Religion" in Warren Goldstein's [ed.] *Marx, Critical Theory, and Religion: A Critique of Rational Choice*. Leiden: Brill.

Ott, Michael R. [ed.] 2007. *The Future of Religion: Toward a Reconciled Society*. Leiden: Brill Academic Publishers.

——. 2009. *The Future of Religion: Toward a Reconciled Society*. Chicago: Haymarket Press.

Otto, Rudolf. 1969. *The Idea of the Holy*. London: Oxford University Press.

——. 1991. *Das Heilige. Über das Irrationale in der Idee des Göttlichen und sein Verhältnis zum Rationalen*. München:Beck.

Parsons, Talcott. 1964. *The System of Modern Societies*. Englewood Cliffs, NJ: Prentice Hall

——. 1965. *Societies: Evolutionary and Comparative Perspectives*, Englewood Cliffs, NJ: Prentice Hall.

——. 1971. "Belief, Unbelief, and Disbelief. " Pp 207-245 in *The Culture of Unbelief: Studies and Proceeding from the First International Symposium on Belief Held at Rome*, March 22-27, 1969, edited by Rocco Caporale and Antonio Grumelli. Berkeley: University of California Press.

Parsons, Talcott and Edward A. Shils. 1951. *Toward a General Theory of Action*. New York: Harper and Row, Publishers.

Peukert, Helmut. 1976. *Wissenschaftstheorie–Handlungstheorie– Fundamentale Theologie. Analysen zu Ansatz und Status Theologischer Theoreibildung*. Dusseldorf: Patmos Verslag.

———. 2009 *Wissenschaftstheorie–Handlungstheorie–Fundamentale Theologie. Analysen zu Ansatz und Status Theologischer Theoreibildung*. Frankfurt a. M. : Suhrkamp Verlag

Pope John XXIII. 1962. *Encyclical Letter: Mater et Magistra*. Vatican. May 15. [www. vatican. va/holy_father/john_xxiii/ encyclicals/index. htm.]

———. 1963. *Pacem in Terris, Rundschreiben uber den Frieden unter allen Volkern in Wahrheit, Gerechtigkeit, Liebe und Freiheit*, Leutesdorf am Rhein: Johannes Verlag.

Popper, Karl R. 1968a. *The Logic of Scientific Discovery*. New York: Basic Books.

———. 1968b. *Conjectures and Refutations: The Growth of Scientific Knowledge*. New York: Harper and Row Publishers.

———. 1969. *The Poverty of Historicism*. London: Routledge and Paul Kegan.

———. 1971. *The Open Society and its Enemies. Volume II. Hegel and Marx*. New Jersey: Princeton University Press.

Prabhupada, Swami. 1974. *Bhagavad-gita As It Is*. London: Collier MacMillan Publishers.

Raines, J. C. and T. Dean [eds.] 1970. *Marxism and Radical Religion: Essays Toward a Revolutionary Humanism*. Philadelphia: Temple University Press.

Reich, Wilhelm. 1971. *The Mass Psychology of Fascism*. New York: Farrar, Straus and Giroux.

———. 1976. *The Murder of Christ*. New York: Pocket Books.

Robinson, John A. T. 1963. *Honest to God*. London: SCM Press

Rosenbaum, Ron. 1998. *Explaining Hitler: Auf der Suche nach dem Ursprung des Bösen–Die Hitler–Debatte*. Hamburg: Europa Verlag.

Rudolphi, Georg, W. 1949. *Heilige Kirche. Kirche der Heiligen*. Frankfurt a. M: Verlag. Jospef Knecht.

Rulff. Dieter. 2011. " Defizite linker Poliotik, " in *Neue Gesellschaft/ Frankfurter Hefte* 5/58

Schachtel, Ernest. 1959. *Metamorphosis*. New York: Basic Books.

Scheible, Hartmut 1989, *Theodor W. Adrno mit Selbstzeugnissen und Bilddokumenten*. Reinbek bei Hamburg: Rowohlt Taschenbuch Verlag.

Scheller, Wolf. 2011. " Zornig bleiben. Max Frisch und die Deutschen", in *Neue Geselschaft/ Frankfurter Hefte* 5/20.

Schelling, Friedrich Wilhelm Joseph von. 1860. *Sämptliche Werke*, Berlin.

———. 1946. *Weltalter. Urfassungen*. München.

———. 1977a. *Philosophische Untersuchungen über das Wesen der menschlichen Freiheit und die damit zusammenhängenden Gegenstände*. Stuttgart: Philipp Reclam.

———. 1977b. *Über das Wesen der menschlichen Freiheit*. Stuttgart: Reclam Philipp

———. 1993. *Philosophie der Offenbarung 1841/1842*.

Schmid-Noerr. Gunzelin. 2000. " Zwischen Sozialpsychologie und Ethik. Erich Fromm und die 'Frankfurter Schule'", in the *Institut für Sozialforschung. An der Johann Wolfgang* Goethe-*Universität*. Frankfurt am Main. Mitteiungen. Heft 11. September.

Schmidt, Helmut. 2011. *Religion in der Verantwortung. Gefährdugen des Friedens im Zeitalter der Globalizierung*. Berlin : Ullstein Buchverlag

Scholem, Gershom. 1935. *Die Geheimnisse der Schöpfung. Ein Kapitel aus dem Sohar*. Berlin.

———. 1967. *Die jüdische Mystik in ihren Hauptströmungden*. Frankfurt a. M. : Suhrkamp Verlag.

———. 1970a. *Judaica II*. Frankfurt a. M. : Suhrkamp Verlag.

———. 1970b. *Über einige Grundbegriffe des Judentums*. Frankfurt a. M. : Suhrkamp Verlag.

———. 1973a. *Judaica III*. Frankfurt a. M. : Suhrkamp Verlag.

———. 1973b. *Zur Kabbala und ihrer Symbolik*. Frankfurt a. M. : Suhrkamp Verlag.

———. 1977a. "Der Nihilismus als religiöses Phänomen, " p. 1-50 in *Eranos Jahrbuch*, Leiden.

———. 1977b. *Von Berlin nach Jerusalem*. Frankfurt a. M. : Suhrkamp Verlag.

———. 1977c. *Von der mystischen Gestalt der Gottheit*. Frankfurt a. M. : Suhrkamp Verlag.

——. 1980. *"… und alles ist Kabbala"* Gershom ·Scholem im Gesprach mit Jorg Drews, München: Edition Text+Kritik.

——. 1982. *Walter Benjamin, The Story of a Friendship*: London: Faber and Faber Ltd.

——. 1989. *The Correspondence of Walter Benjamon und Gerschom Scholem 1932–1940*. New York: Schocken Books.

Schopenhauer, Arthur. 1946. *Aphorismen zur Lebensweischeit*. Wiesbaden: Brockhaus Verlag.

——. 1977. *Die Welt als Wille und Vorstellung II*. Zürich: Diogenes Verlag.

——. 1989. *Sämptliche Werke* Frankfurt a. M. : Suhrkamp Verlag.

Schwan, Hesine/ Thymian Bussemer . 2011. "Der Wert der repräsentativen Demokratie, " in *Neue Gesellschaft/ Frankfurter Hefte* 5/58.

Siebert, Rudolf, J. 1965. *Die Anthropologie Michael Heldings, eines Humanisten und Theologen* im Umkreis der Geistigen Neuordnung des 16. Jahrhunderts (1506-1561). Sigmaringen:Hohenzollernsche Jahreshefte.

—— 1966. "A German Experience, " in *At the Cross Road*, 5 (2 and 3):12-14.

——. 1978. "Communication without Domination, " in G. Baum und A. Greeley [eds.] *Communication in the Church*. NewYork: The Seabury Press (Concilium. Religion in the Seventies).

——. 1979a. *From Critical Theory of Society to Theology of Communicative Praxis*. Lanham, MD: University Press of America.

——. 1979b. *Hegel's Concept of Marriage and Family: The Origin of Subjective Freedom*. Washington, D. C. : University Press of America.

——. 1979c. *Hegel's Philosophy of History: Theological, Humanistic and Scientific Elements*. Washington, D. C. : University Press of America.

——. 1979d. *Horkheimer's Critical Sociology of Religion: The Relative and the Transcendent*. Washington, D. C. : University Press of America.

——. 1979e. "The Future of Marrage and Family: Withering away ior Restructuring, " in A. Greeley [ed.] in *The Family in Crisis or Transition. A Sociological and Theological Perspective.*

New York: The Seabury Press. (Concilium: Religion in the Seventies).

——. 1980. "Parson's Analytical Theory of Religion as Ultimate Reality, " in Gregory Baum [ed.], *Sociology and Human Destiny*. New York: Seabury Press.

——. 1985. *Critical Theory of Religion: The Frankfurt School – From Universal Pragmatic to Political Theology*. Berlin: Mouton Publishers, a Division of Walter de Gruyter & Co.

——. 1986. "Marriage and Eucharist and Socialism, " in *Cross Currents*, (39) 4: 442–457.

——. 1987a. *From Critical Theory of Society to Theology of Communicative Praxis*. Lewiston, NY: Edwin Mellen Press.

——. 1987b. *Hegel's Philosophy of History: Theological, Humanistic and Scientific Elements*. Lewiston, NY: Edwin Mellen Press.

——. 1987c. *Hegel's Concept of Marriage and Family: The Origin of Subjective Freedom*. Lewiston, NY: Edwin Mellen Press.

——. 1987d. *Horkheimer's Critical Sociology of Religion: The Relative and the Transcendent*. Lewiston, NY: Edwin Mellen Press.

——. 1989. *From Critical Theory to Communicative Political Theology: Universal Solidarity*. New York: Peter Lang Publishing.

——. 1993. *Recht, Macht und Liebe: Georg W. Rudolphi's Prophetische Politische Theologie*. Frankfurt a. M. : Haag and Herchen.

——. 1994a. *Critical Reflections on the Dialectical Relationship between Theology and Religiology, and other Human and Social Sciences*. New Brunswick, Canada: St. Thomas University Press.

——. 1994b. "Frankfurt to Dubrovnik: An Interview with Rudolf Siebert" by Stewart Donovan. *The Nashwaak Review*, Vol. 1 (Fall):69–90.

——. 1994c. *From Critical Theory to Critical Political Theology: Personal Autonomy and Universal Solidarity*. New York: Peter Lang Publishing.

——. 1994d. *The Dialectic of Revelation and Autonomous Reason*. Fredericton: St. Thomas University.

——. 1995. *Kant, Hegel, and Habermas on War and Peace*. Joannina

——. 2000. "Transcendence without Counter–Movement In and After Auschwitz. " [www.rudolfjsiebert. org/ web_publications. htm.]

——. 2001. *The Critical Theory of Religion: The Frankfurt School*: Lanham, MD: The Scarecrow Press.

———. 2002a. *From Critical Theory to Political Theology: Personal Autonomy and Universal Solidarity.* New York: Peter Lang Publishing.

———. 2002b. "The Future of Religion: The Rescue of Religious Motives and Motivations through their Inverstion into Secular Discourse, " in *Traditional Religion and Culture in a New Era,* Reimon Bachika [ed.] New Brunswick: Transaction Publishers.

———. 2002c. "The Open Dialectic of Jewish, Christian and Islamic Monotheism and Radical Enlightenment: Toward a Global Ethos of Autonomy and Solidarity" *in Religion in Civil Society, Materials of the III International Seminar, November in Yalta,* Tatyana A. Senyushkina [ed.]. Simferopol: Tauria.

———. 2003. "Toward a Critical Theory of Religion: The Longing for the Totally Other. " in *Religion and Civil Society Materials of the IV International Seminar November in Yalta,* Tatyana A. Senyushkina [ed.] Simferopol: Tauria.

———. 2004a. "La théorie critique de la religion de Theodor Adorno: théologie inverse contre clérico-fascisme, " in *X–Alta¸ Terreur et Sacralité.* Novembre, Number 8. Abjat/Bandiat, France.

———. 2004b. "The Open Dialectic between Religious and Secular Values and Norms: The Course of Civilization in the 21st Century" in *Religious Innovation in a Global Age: Essays on the Construction of Spirituality,* George N. Lundskow [ed.] Jefferson, NC: McFarland & Co.

———. 2004c. Interview with Gregory Baum in the Airport of Montreal, Canada, on August 15. (unpublished) .

———. 2005a. "Frankfurt to Kalamazoo to Dubrovnik & Jalta: A Biographical Story. " *Critical Theory of Society and Religion: Home Page of Professor Rudolf J. Siebert,* [www. rudolfjsiebert. org/bio_story. htm.]

———. 2005b. *Le Relatif et le Transcendant: la sociologie critique de la religion de Max Horkheimer.* Translated from English by Fabien Ollier and Henri Vaugrand. Paris: L'Harmattan.

———. 2005c. "Toward a Discourse between Cognitive and Critical Theoreticians of Religion: Open Dialectic between the Religious and the Secular" in *Religion as Human Capacity : A Festschrift in Honor of E. Thomas Lawson,* Timothy Light and Brian Wilson [eds.] Leiden: Brill Academic Publishers.

——. 2005d. "The Critical Theory of Society: The Longing for the Totally Other, " in *Critical Sociology,* Volume 31/Number 1-2: 57-114.

——. 2005e. "The Critical Theory of Religion: Critical Religion in Antagonistic Civil Society, "in *Religion and Civil Society. Materials of the VI International Seminar November in Yalta,* Tatyana A. Senyushkina [ed.] Simferopol: Tauria.

——. 2005f. "The Critical Theory of Religion: Towards Discourse and Cooperation among Civilizations" in *Religion and Civil Society Materials of the VI International Seminar 8-10, November 2007 in Yalta,* Tatyana A. Senyushkina [ed.] Simferopol: Tauria.

——. 2006a. *Lex Talionis: Religion, force et terreur – suivi der Thomas Müntzer: Jus Talionis,* introduction by Henri Vaugrand. Abjat Sur Bandiat, France: X–Alta

——. 2006b. "Liberation et redemption dans la musique Hegel–Horkheimer–Adorno. " in *X–Alta. Musicopathie del'impossibilite de la musique.* Numero 9, decembre. Abjat/Bandiat, France.

——. 2006c. "The Critical Theory of Religion: Toward an Open Dialectic Between Religious Faith and Secular Experience and Knowledge, " *Forum on Public Policy,* 2 (1): 1-32.

——. 2006d. "Toward a Dialectical Sociology of Religion: A Crique of Positivism and Clerico–Fascism" in *Marx, Critical Theory, and Religion: A Critque of Rational Choice,* Warren S. Goldstein [ed.] Leiden: Brill Academic Publishers.

——. 2007a. "Our Friendship: It began with Thomas Müntzer, the Theologian of Revolution" in *Creed and Conscience: Essays in Honor of A. James Reimer,* edited by Jeremy M Bergen, Paul G. Doerksen, and Karl Koop. Toronto: Pandora Press.

——. 2007b. "Theology of Revolution versus Theology of Counter–Revolution" in *The Futurof Religion: Toward a Reconciled Society,* Michael R. Ott [ed.] Leiden: Brill Academic Publishers.

——. 2007c. "The Critical Theory of Religion: The Evolution of the Moral Consciousness from the Jus Talionis to the Golden Rule. " A paper given at the International Society for the Sociology of Religion Conference, Jul. 25, Leipzig, Germany. (Unpublished).

——. 2007d. "The Critical Theory of Religion: The Golden Rule. " Paper given at Saint Petersburg University, Saint Petersburg.

Russia, November 6. From Russian Website: [http:peacefromharmony. org].

——. 2007e. "The Critical Theory of Religion: New Models. " A paper given at Saint Petersburg University, Saint Petersburg. Russia, November 6. From Russian Website: [http:peacefromharmony. org].

——. 2007f. "The Development of the Critical Theory of Religion in Dubrovnik from 1975 to 2007, " in *The Future of Religion: Toward a Reconciled Society*, Michael R. Ott [ed.], Leiden: Brill.

——. 2007g. "Erinnerung an den Christen und Humanisten Otto Schuhmann im Kontext der Barbarei" in A. Askenasy's [ed.] *Otto Schuhmann 1888–1950, Ein Schulmeister in den Zerreissproben seiner Zeit*, New York: A. Askenasy Publisher.

——. 2008a. "The Critical Theory of Religion: Jus Talionis, " in *Religion and Civil Society:* Identity Crisis and New Challenges of Post-Secular Society . Materials of the VII *International Seminar 8-10, November 2007 in Yalta*, Tatyana A. Senyushkina [ed.] Simferopol: Tauria.

——. 2008b. "The Jesus Revolution, the Judas Kiss, and the Empires, " (Russian) in *Religion* and Civil Society: Identity Crisis and New Challenges of Post-Secular Society . Materials *of the VII International Seminar 8-10 November, 2007, in Yalta*, Tatyana A. Senyushkina [ed.] Simferopol: Tauria.

——. 2008c. "St. Petersburg – Yalta Report" in *Proceedings of VII International Seminar, November 8-10, 2007. Yalta*. Tatyana A. Senyushkina [ed.] Svastopol, NPCEKOST-2008d. "The Jesus Revolution, the Judas Kiss, and the Empires, " in *X–Alta*, Abjat/Bandiat, France. [in process of publication.]

——. 2008e. "Dialectical Reliogiology: The Expansion and Contraction of God, " in Proceedings of VIII International Seminar, November 19-22. Yalta. Tatyana A. Senyushkina [ed.] Sevastopol, NPCEKOST .

——. 2008f. "Dialectical Reliogiology: Religious Hope and the Defaitism of Modern Reason, "in *Proceedings of VIII International Seminar, November 19-22. Yalta.* Tatyana A. Senyushkina [ed.] Sevastopol, NPCEKOST .

——. 2009a. *Dialectical Religiology: Hitler's Theodicy and the Suffering of the People* (Work in Preparation.)

——. 2009d. "Religiöser Glaube und Säkulare Vernunft: Offenbarung und Aufklärung, " in *Religion als Lebensmacht*. Leipzig: Evangelische Verlagsanstalt.

——. 2009e. "Dialectical Religiology I: Against Aggression, Force, Violence, & Terror. " A paper given at the 33rd International Course on the Future of Religion: Mutual Treatment of Believing and Non-believing Citizens. IUC. Dubrovnik Croatia. April/May. (Unpublished).

——. 2009f. "Dialectical Religiology II: From Monotheism, through Atheism to Humanistic Post-Theism". A paper given at the 33rd International Course on the Future of Religion: Mutual Treatment of Believing and Non-believing Citizens". IUC. Dubrovnik Croatia. April/May. (Unpublished.)

——. 2009g. "Dialectical Religiology III: The Jewish-German Tragedy. " A paper given at the 33rd International Course on the Future of Religion: Mutual Treatment of Believing and Non-believing Citizens". IUC. Dubrovnik Croatia. April/May. (Unpublished.

——. 2009h. "Dialectical Religiology IV: German Nationalism and Zionism". A paper given at the 33rd International Course on the Future of Religion: Mutual Treatment of Believing and Non-believing Citizens". IUC. Dubrovnik Croatia. April/May. (Unpublished).

——. 2009i. "Dialectical Religiology: The Future of Religion. " ISCSCC Conference.

——. 2009j: *Dialectical Religiology: A Family Story.* (Work in Preparation.)

——. 2009k. " Dialectical Religiology: The Future of Religion:, in Farhat-Holzmann, Laina/Thomas Rienzo, *Civilization in Crisis*. Western Michigan University. Kalamazoo, Michigan. USA June 3-7.

——. 2010a. "Religiöser Glaube und Säkulare Vernunft: Offenbarung und Aufklärung, "in Thomas Bohrmann und Jochen Bohn. *Religion als Lebensmacht* Leipzig:Evangelische Verlagsanstalt., Pp. 237-247.

——. -2010b. Manifesto of the Critical Theory of Society and Religion:The Wholly Other, *Liberation, Happiness and the Rescue of the Hopeless.* Leiden : Brill Publisher, Vol, I, II, III

———. 2010c2010c. "The Development of the Critical Theory of Society and Religion : The Yearning for Perfect Justice and Unconditional Love: Chapter in *Critical Sociologyy*, Teheran 2010 (Book)

———. 2010d. " The Evolution of the Dialectical Religiology: Longing that the Murderer shall not triumph over the innocnt Victim. " Article in *Critical Sociology* Teheran 2010. (Journal)

———. *2010e.* "The Roke of Religionin Civilizational Development in the last 6000 Years, " Chapter in book of the *International Society for the Comparative Srudy of Civilizations,*

———. 2010f. "Are there Common Values in Various Religion. " Chapter in book of *The International Society for the Comparatve Study of Civilizations, :*

———. 2010g. "The Dialectical Religiology: The Civilizational Function of Religion. From the Ancient Mesopotamia and Egypt to the Modern and Post-Modern Europe and America" in *Religion and Civil Society Materials of the VI International Seminar November in Yalta,* Tatyana A. Senyushkina [ed.] Simferopol: Tauria.

———. 2011a. "The Dialectical Religiology: The Civilizational Function of Religion. From the Ancient Mesopotamia and Egypt to the Modern and Post-Modern Europe and America" in *Religion and Civil Society Materials of the VI International Seminar November in Yalta,* Tatyana A. Senyushkina [ed.] Simferopol: Tauria.

———2011b. "The Devekopment of the Critical Theory of Society and Religion:The Yearning for Perfect Justice and Unconditional Love. " In *Islamic Perspective.* Volume 5.

Siri, Jasmin. 2011. " Internet und Demokratisierung, " in *Neue Gesellschaft/ Frankfurter Hefte* 5/58.

Smith. Jesse M. 2011. " Becoming an Atheist in America: Constructing Identity and Meaning from the Rejection of Theism, " In *Sociology of Relgion. A Quarterly Review.* Volume 72. No. 2. Summer 2011.

Snyder, Timothy. 2011. "A New Aprroach to the Holocaus. " In *The New York Review.* May

Sölle, Dorothy. 1977. *Revolutionary Patience.* Maryknoll, NY: Orbis Books.

———. 1992. *Gott im Müll, Eine andere Entdeckung latein Amerika's.* Mücnhen: Deutscher Taschenbuch Verlag.

———. 1994. *Atheistisch an Gott glauben, Beitruage zur Theologie.* München: Deutscher Taschenbuch Verlag.

Sölle, Dorothee, Jürgen Habermas, et al. 1975. *Religionsgespräche. Zur gesellschaftlichen Rolle der Religion.* Darmstadt; Herrmann Luchterhand Verlag.

Sölle, Dorothy and Johannes B. Metz. 1990. *Welches Christentum hat Zukunft, D. Sölle und J. B*   *. Metz im Gespräch mit K. J. Kuschel.* Stuttgart: Kreuz Verlag.

SorosGeorge. 2011. " My Philanthropy, " In The New York Review, " May.

Spencer, Robert. 2011. *"Egypt Comes Out for Hamas",* in *Right Side News* 27. May, 1-2.

Stiegnitz, Peter. 2011. " Ungarn verabschiedet sich von der Demokratie., " in *Neue Gesellschaft/ Frankfurter Hefte* 5/58.

Stone, Ronald H. /Matthew, Lon Weaver (eds). 1998. Against the Third Reich. Paul Tillich's Wartime Radio Broadcasts into Nazi Germany. Luisville Kentucky: Westminster John Knox Press.

The Holy Qur'an. 1934. Translation and Commentary by A. Yusuf Ali. The Holy Koran Publishing House

Thierse, Wolfgang. 2011. "Erinnerung an Walter Dirks, ", " in *Neue Gesellschaft/ Frankfurter Hefte* 5/58.

Thomas Aquinas 1922. *Summa Contra Gentiles seu De Veritate Catholicae Fidei.* Taurini (Italia):Ex Officina Libraria Marietti anno 1820 condita.

Tillich, Paul. 1926. *Kairos II. Ideen zur Geisteslage der Gegenwart* in Gesammelte Werke. Vol. 6. Frankfurt a. M. 1962.

———. 1929. *Religious Realization.* Berlin.

———. 1933. *The Socalist Decision.* Potsdam

———. 1948. *The Shaking of the Foundations.* New York: Charles Scribner's Sons.

———. 1951. *Systematic Theology: Volume 1.* Chicago, Illinois: The University of Chicago Press.

———. 1952. *The Courage to Be.* New Haven, Conneticut: Yale University Press.

———. 1955a. *The New Being.* New York: Charles Scribner's Sons.

——. 1955b. *Biblical Religion and the Search for Ultimate Reality.* Chicago: University of Chicago Press.

——. 1957. *Systematic Theology: Volume 2.* Chicago, Illinois: The University of Chicago Press.

——. 1963a. *Systematic Theology: Volume 3.* Chicago: Illinois: The University of Chicago Press.

——. 1963b. *Morality and Beyond.* New York: Harper and Row.

——. 1966. *On the Boundary.* New York: Charles Scribner's Sons.

——. 1972. *The Courage to Be.* New Haven, Conneticut: Yale University Press.

——. 1977. *The Socialist Decision.* New York: Harper and Row.

——. 1983. *The Socialist Decision.* Washington D. C. : University Press of America.

Vahanian, Gabriel. 1967. *The Death of God: The Culture of Our Post–Christian Era.* New York: Geroge Braziller——.

——. 1977. *God and Utopia. The Church in a Technological Civilization.* New York : The Seabury Pres

Weber, Max. 1952. *Ancient Judaism.* New York: Free Press.

——. 1962. *Basic Concepts in Sociology.* New York: The Citadel Press.

——. 1963. *The Sociology of Religion.* Boston: Beacon Press.

——. 1969. *The Theory of Social and Economic Organization.* New York: The   Free Press.

——. 1978. *Economy and Society: An Outline of Interpretive Sociology,* 2 Volumes. Berkeley:University of California Press.

——. 1992. "The Protestant Sects and the Spirit of Capitalism, " in *From Max Weber: Essays in Sociology,* trans. and ed. by Hans H. Gerth and C. Wright Mills, New York: Oxford University Press.

——. 2002. "'Churches' and 'Sects' in North America, " in Max Weber, *The Protestant Ethics and the "Spirit of Capitalism" and Other Writings.* New York:Penguin Books.

Weitensteiner, Hans K. 2002. *Warum denn wir, immer wir. . ? War diese Stadt Frankfurt schuldiger als London?: Katholisches Gemeindeleben im Dritten Reich und während der ersten Nachkriegsjahre 1932–1950. Dokumente und Darstellung.* Frankfurt a. M. : Haag and Herchen.

Wiesel, Elie. 1982. *Night.* New York: Bantam Books.

——. 1992. *The Forgotten.* New York: Schocken Books.

Williams Rhys H. 2011. " 2010 Association for the Sociology of Religion Presidential AddressCreating an American Islam: Thoughts on Religion, Identity and Place . " In *Sociology of Religion. A Quarterly Review.* Volume 72. Nio 2. Summer 2011.

Wolf. Michael. 2000. " Psychoanalyse als Forschugsmethode. Der Beitrag von Erich Fromm" in the *Institut für Sozialforschung. An der Johann Wolfgang Goethe- Universität.* Frankfurt am Main. *Mitteilungen.* Heft 11. September

Zizek, Slavoj. 2007. "Resistance is Surrender. " *London Review of Books.* November 15, 29 (22). [www. lrb. co. uk/v29/n22/zize01. html.]

———. 2009. *First as Tragedy, Then as Farce.* London:Verso.

Zizek, Slavoj and John Milbank. 2008. *The Monstrosity of Christ: Paradox or Dialectic?* Cambridge, Massachusetts: The MIT Press.

Zizek, Slavoj/Clayton Crocket/Creston Davis (eds). 1011. *Hegel and the Infinite. Religion, Politics, and Dialectic.* New York: Columbia University Press.

Zöpel, Christoph. 011. "Globale und europ¥ische Demokratie, " in *Neue Gesellschaft/ Frankfurter Hefte* 5/58